# FORWARD

The greatest act a Christian can do
Is to worship God in Spirit and in Truth.
All endeavors for God must begin here.
The Scriptures teach us that God seeks three things:
1. Those who will worship Him in Spirit and in Truth. (John 4:23)
2. Glory (John 8:50)
3. The lost (Luke 19:10)

In Heaven there is continuous worship in the atmosphere of God's Glory.
Worshiping God in His Spirit and in His Truth
Brings His manifest Presence and His Glory,
Because God lives in the praise and worship of His people.
His manifest Presence and Glory, brings His Kingdom to earth as in Heaven
When His Kingdom comes to earth as in Heaven, His will is done
And the work of the devil is destroyed;
The devil must stand down, stand back and depart.
Christ Jesus admonished His disciples to seek first and above all His Kingdom.

Where His Kingdom comes to earth as in Heaven, Christ Jesus rules and reigns;
Where Christ Jesus rules and reigns
There is continuous victory for the people of God, The Bride of Christ.
All the lost who hear the call of God
Are drawn to His Presence and Glory like moths to a flame.

The Day of Pentecost began a never ending Revival.
A Revival brought about by Christ, the Holy Spirit entering into
And living in His people and the outworking of this phenomenon.
Every subsequent revival has its origin in The Day of Pentecost.
Every subsequent revival has had the characteristics of The Day of Pentecost
Because Christ Jesus is "The Charismatic," "The Inventor of Pentecost."
The Final Revival lies immediately ahead;
Christ Jesus will confirm a covenant with His Bride for three and one half years;
For three and one-half years She will minister in His fullness,
Revealing Christ in all His Glory, in every nation of the face of the earth.
The name of Jesus will be upon every heart, mind and mouth,
Every man woman and child.
The hallmark of this Revival will be
The Bride of Christ worshiping Her God in His Spirit and in his Truth.

Just as with the the coming of Christ Jesus in His day,
The Bride of Christ will cause the falling and rising of many
Who claim the name of Christ, and will be a name spoken against,
So that the thoughts of many hearts will be revealed,
Just as Simeon prophesied of Christ Jesus. (Luke 2:34-35)

# INTRODUCTION

Today, Christ Jesus is calling forth His Bride in this generation (A paraphrase form the Song of Songs put into poetic form):

Arise my darling my beautiful One
Arise my darling my beautiful One, come with Me
The winter is past and the rains are all gone
The flowers appear, the time for singing has come

Arise and come with Me
Arise and come, arise and come,
Arise and come with Me

The cooing of doves is heard in our land
The fig tree forms its early fruit
The blossoming vines spread their fragrance

Arise and come with Me
Arise and come, arise and come,
Arise and come with Me

The Bride of Christ as seen by Christ Jesus
(A paraphrase form the Song of Songs put into poetic form):

Who is this that appears like the dawn
Fair as the moon bright as the sun
Majestic as the stars, all beautiful you are
There is no flaw in you

You have stolen My heart my sister My Bride
With one glance of your eyes

How delightful is your love my darling
Better than wine, fragrant as perfume
You are a garden fountain, a well of flowing water
There is no one like you

You have stolen My heart my sister My Bride
With one glance of your eyes

Your King is captivated by your beauty
Your King is captivated by you

# WORSHIP GOD IN SPIRIT AND IN TRUTH

*From the lips of children and infants you have ordained praise*
*Because of your enemies,*
*To silence the foe and the avenger. (Psalm 8:2)*

## The Purpose of God In Creation
The purpose of God in creation was to obtain a Bride for His Son;
A Bride who of Her own free will would choose to marry His Son;
A Bride who would be commensurate with His Son in character and being;
A Bride who would love His Son as He loved His Son;
A Bride who would become ONE with His Son by the power of His Holy Spirit.
A Bride with whom His Son could enjoy intimate communion for eternity.
A Bride who will worship Him in Spirit and in Truth.
This purpose of God is the framework for all of Scriptural history.
When this Bride worships her God in Spirit and in Truth
She brings forth the manifest Presence of God
Then the world knows that Christ Jesus was sent by the Father to the earth.

## In The New Covenant God Seeks Three Things
1. Those who will worship Him in Spirit and in Truth. (John 4:23)
2. Glory (John 8:50)
3. The lost (Luke 19:10)

It seems only reasonable that the Church of God would endeavor
To give to their God what He seeks when it is possible for them to do so.
When the people of God worship Him in Spirit and in Truth;
That is in and through Christ in them,
He releases His manifest, tangible Presence and Glory;
Which takes over the whole spiritual atmosphere;
Bringing the Kingdom of God to earth as in Heaven
And a God consciousness in believers and unbelievers.
Then all know assuredly that Christ Jesus was sent as their Lord and Savior.
Today, as in every preceding generation,
Christ Jesus is seeking those  who will worship Him in Spirit and in Truth,
Who love Him with all their heart, soul, mind and strength
So that the whole world will know that He was sent by God the Father.

## True Worshipers
Jesus said to the woman at the well:
*Believe me woman, a time is coming*
*When you will worship the Father neither on this mountain nor in Jerusalem.*

4

<u>Worship God In Spirit And In Truth</u>

*You Samaritans worship what you do not know;*
*We worship what we do know;*
*For salvation is from the Jews.*
*Yet a time is coming and has now come*
*When the true worshipers will worship the Father in Spirit and in Truth,*
*For they are the kind of worshipers the Father seeks.*
*God is Spirit, and his worshipers must worship in Spirit and in Truth. (John 4:21-24)*

When the people of God worship in Spirit and in Truth,
They are worshiping in and through Christ, who is the Spirit, who is the Truth;
Then God manifests Himself.
It is not a specific place; it can be any place where this occurs.
When the people of God worship Him in His Spirit and in His Truth;
Through Christ in them; having been born again of His Spirit;
Then He reveals His manifest Presence and Glory.
The Bride of Christ is compelled by Christ in her
To worship in Spirit and in Truth.

## Your Kingdom Come On Earth As In Heaven
The Lord taught His disciples how to pray,
Your Kingdom come to earth as in Heaven;
The Kingdom where Christ Jesus rules and reigns.
Christ Jesus desires to rule and reign in His people, His Bride.
Finally, in the Millennium, and thereafter
He will rule and reign forever, over all creation; He will extinguish sin.
However, in the here and now, He desires to reign not only in Heaven,
But in and through His Bride
And throughout history He has reigned in His Bride;
Those who consecrated their lives to Him;
Those who gave up their lives to obtain His LIFE.

From Scripture we can see that in Heaven there is continuous worship.
Worship brings the Kingdom of God,
Because God "inhabits" the praises of His people.
The Bride of Christ brings the Kingdom of God to earth as in Heaven
When the She worships God as it is done in Heaven.
This is what occurred in The Tabernacle of David and is our example.
The Psalms, many of which were born out of the Tabernacle of David,
Are our teacher.
When the Kingdom of God comes to earth as in Heaven,
The devil is excluded, his work destroyed.
The devil has no access to the Kingdom of God;
When the Kingdom of God comes to earth as in Heaven
The Presence and Glory of God are manifested unhindered
By the evil, demonic principalities and powers in the heavenly realms.

The primary objective of God on earth is to raise up a Bride for His Son;

A Bride who will become ONE with Him by the power of His Spirit in Her.
A Bride who will worship Him in Spirit and in Truth,
**Then His Kingdom comes to earth as in Heaven,**
**As He is "enthroned" on, or "inhabits" the praises of His people.**
Then His Kingdom Comes to earth as in Heaven;
Then Christ Jesus rules and reigns on earth as in Heaven
And the prayer He taught His disciples is answered.
The Bride of Christ seeks the Kingdom of God above all else
As Christ Jesus admonished;
He placed it within in her, the Holy Spirit in her, Christ in her,
But it only has value as it is made manifest and demonstrated,
As can be seen from the Book of Acts.

## Seek First The Kingdom Of God
Christ Jesus taught His disciples to seek first and above all else The Kingdom of God.
The Kingdom where Christ Jesus rules and reigns;
Where His Presence is manifested; where the devil is shut out.
Access to His Presence, to His Kingdom, is worship in Spirit and in Truth.

## God is Enthroned On The Praises Of His People
*But you are holy, **enthroned** in the praises of Israel* (The Bride of Christ)
*(Psalm 22:3)*

[The Spirit Filled LIFE Bible, New King James Version
Says the following about this verse:
22:3 - Since God is enthroned in the praises,
Worship is the key to entering fully into His presence.
The concept here is that praise releases God's glory,
Thus bringing to the worshipers actualized responses of His kingly reign.
His enthroned responses through the Holy Spirit can take many forms,
such as prophecy, healings, miracles, affirmation to individual hearts,
A call to reverential silence and awe, conviction of sin, and salvation of sinners.
**This verse should be a guiding goal**
**For all personal and corporate worship times.**

**22:3 - Praise, the Pathway to God's Presence,** PRAISE PATHWAY.
Unquestionably, one of the most remarkable an exciting things about honest
And sincere praise is taught here:
Praise will bring the presence of God.
Although God is everywhere present, there is a distinct manifestation of His rule,
Which enters the environment of praise.
Here is the remedy for times when you feel depressed.
Praise! However simply, compose your song and testimony
Of God's goodness in your life.
The result: God enters! His presence will live (take up residence) in our lives.
The word "inhabit" (Hebrew yawshab) means
"To sit down, to remain, to settle, or marry."

<u>Worship God In Spirit And In Truth</u>

In other words, God does not merely visit us when we praise Him,
But His presence abides with us
And we partner with him in a growing relationship!
Let this truth create faith and trust,
And lead to deliverance from satanic harassments, torment, or bondage.
Notice how this text ties three words together: "praises," "trusted," and "delivered"!]

## Meetings Consecrated By His Glory

The primary purpose in Christians gathering together
Should be the same as it was in the days of Moses
And the original Tent of Meeting, the "prototype" for the Church today;
**That is to meet with God, that He might speak to us.**
When we meet for this primary purpose,
**Then God will consecrate the meeting by His Glory;**
**Then He will dwell in our midst;**
Then we will know that He is our God who brought us out of Egypt;
Then we are differentiated from all the other peoples of the earth;
Then the peoples of the earth will know where to come to meet with God;
In the midst of the people of God; in the midst of His Glory.

*For generations to come this burnt offering* (worship) *is to be made regularly*
*At the entrance to the Tent of Meeting before the Lord.*
***There I will meet you and speak to you;***
***There I will meet with the Israelites,***
***<u>And the place will be consecrated by my glory.</u>***

***So I will consecrate the Tent of Meeting and the altar and will consecrate***
***Aaron and his sons to serve me as priests.***
***Then I will dwell among the Israelites and be their God.***
***They will know that I am the Lord their God, who brought them out of Egypt***
***So that I might dwell among them.***
***I am the Lord their God.*** *(Exodus 29:42-46)*

It is the desire of God to meet and speak with us,
To consecrate our meetings with His glory;
Then His Kingdom comes to earth as in Heaven;
Then it is clear who belongs to God and who does not;
Then the people He calls by His Spirit know where to come to meet Him;
Then He adds people to His Bride according to His will.
**The whole purpose of "Church" or assembling together**
**Is so that God can meet with us, speak to us and add to us.**

## What does A New Covenant Assembly Look Like?

The apostle Paul describes this:

*When you come together, everyone has a hymn, or a word of instruction,*

<u>Worship God In Spirit And In Truth</u>

*A revelation, a tongue or an interpretation.*
*All of these must be done for the strengthening of the church.*
*If anyone speaks in a tongue, two—or at the most three—should speak,*
*One at a time, and someone must interpret.*
*If there is no interpreter, the speaker should keep quiet in the church*
*And speak to himself and God.*

*Two or three prophets should speak,*
*And the others should weigh carefully what is said.*
*And if a revelation comes to someone who is sitting down,*
*The first speaker should stop.*
*For you can all prophesy in turn*
*So that everyone may be instructed and encouraged.*
*The spirits of prophets are subject to the control of prophets.*
*For God is not a God of disorder but of peace. (1 Corinthians 14:26-33)*

The meetings of The Bride of Christ will follow this pattern.

## The House of Praise Was At The Entrance To The Tabernacle

In the layout of the tribes of Israel around the Tabernacle of Moses,
The House of Praise, the Tribe of Judah,
Was positioned at the entrance to the Tabernacle.
Even the tents of Moses and Aaron were outside of the Tribe of Judah.
This was God speaking eloquently about the importance of praise
In the Old Covenant and its fulfillment in the New Covenant,
Praise is central to worship.
Access through His gates and into His courts is praise.
Access to the Holy Place and the Holy of Holies is intimate worship,
A sweet smelling incense, from a consecrated people.
The heart of God is to manifest His Presence through a consecrated people.

## When We Meet With God Our Face Will Shine

When Moses met with God his face shone with the Glory of God.
God wants the face of His Church to shine with the Glory of God.
When Steven testified for God his face shone with the Glory of God;
He looked like and angel;
When you stand in the Presence of God your face will shine with His Glory.
The Bride of Christ will shine with the Glory of God.

## When You Meet With God You Will Be Forever Changed

God's manifest Presence changes everyone present.
**Abraham** heard from God and was willing to leave his homeland
And go to a place he never knew.
God changed Abraham's name and his destiny with a covenant.
**Jacob** wrestled with God and had his name and his nature changed;
God gave him a permanent physical mark of that meeting.

**8**

**Moses** met God and was commissioned with a task and destiny;
To deliver Israel from Egypt.
He was changed from shepherd to deliverer.
**David** met God and had only one desire in life; to be in His Presence;
He was changed from shepherd to king, psalmist and prophet.
**On the Day of Pentecost**, the Church met God and were intoxicated with His Glory,
Spoke in languages they did not know,
And went on to change the world through Christ in them.
When God met you, you were changed from being dead, to being alive in Christ.
You can now do exceedingly and abundantly above what you can think or ask
Because of the power of Christ in you.

## Access To The Presence Of God:
## The Mercy Seat,
## Which Was Over The Ark Of His Presence,
## In The Most Holy Place
The Mercy Seat provides our only approach to God.
Because it has been sprinkled with the blood of Christ,
The same blood we have applied to our lives having received Christ by faith.
The Mercy Seat, sprinkled with the blood of Christ Jesus
Allows God to meet with us and speak to us.

## Access To The Most Holy Place
The sacrifice of praise and thanksgiving allows us to enter the courts of God,
And place our offering on the Brazen Altar,
But the Mercy Seat, where God speaks to us, is in the Most Holy Place.
To get to the Most Holy Place we must enter the Holy Place.
To enter the Holy Place we must be a priest, consecrated to God,
Washed, anointed, clothed with Christ and sprinkled and applied with His blood.
To enter the Most Holy Place we must then offer sacred incense, acceptable to God;
True worship from our hearts that touches His heart;
Worship in Spirit and in Truth.

## We Know That Our Worship Has Touched The Heart Of God
## When He Speaks To Us And Reveals His Presence And Glory
That is God's way of acknowledging that our worship has reached Him,
And is acceptable to Him.
God lives in the praises of His people;
We become ONE with Him as we praise and then worship Him;
We are transformed by the words of our mouth, coming from our hearts;
We may begin in the natural but we then allow Christ in us to take over,
Which allows us to enter the supernatural, the realm of the Spirit of God;
The Glory realm of God.

## Worship God In Spirit And In Truth

In the Book of Revelation the apostle John said
That he was "in the Spirit" on the Lord's day.
In this condition, Christ Jesus was able to speak to him
And give him a great revelation; the Book of Revelation.
Praise and Worship enables us to get "in the Spirit;"
When we are "in the Spirit" God can speak to us as He desires.
To hear from God we must get "in the Spirit."
All those "in the Spirit" are ONE with God and each other.

When we are in the Glory realm of God
He manifests His Presence and Glory;
He speaks to us, He communes with us, He loves on us and we love on Him.
In the atmosphere of His Presence and Glory sinners come to Christ Jesus;
Then the sick are healed and the dead are raised.
All things are possible and come to pass in the Glory realm of God.
In the atmosphere of the Presence and Glory of God the devil is driven out.

**We must not satisfy ourselves with glimpses of His Presence and Glory.**
God wants to immerse us in His Glory continually;
He wants us to live in "The Secret Place of the Most High God;"
He wants His Kingdom to come to earth as in Heaven and reside there, continually.
His objective is that we become ONE with Him and live in His Presence.
**We need to press into worship**
**Until we are immersed in His Presence and Glory.**

True worship lifts Christ up and allows God to manifest His Presence;
Then He draws all men to Himself;
This is New Covenant evangelism and the Glory He is seeking;
God is glorified when His people worship Him in Spirit and in Truth;
God is glorified when people accept His Christ as their Lord and Savior
Every Christian can participate in this most glorious enterprise;
**No one is excluded; nothing is more important.**

## The Bride Of Christ Will Join With David In Asking But One Thing

*One thing I ask, this is what I seek*
*That I may dwell in the house of the Lord*
*All the days of my life*
*To gaze upon the beauty of the Lord*
*And seek Him in His temple. (Psalm 27:4)*

*Whom have I in Heaven but you?*
*And being with you, I desire nothing on earth. (Psalm 73:25)*

*I said to the Lord, 'You are my Lord;*
*Apart from you I have no good thing.' (Psalm 16:2)*

<u>Worship God In Spirit And In Truth</u>

As God Seeks those who will worship Him in Spirit and in Truth,
The Bride of Christ seeks to worship Him who is the Spirit and the Truth;
To gaze upon the beauty of the Lord
And they become ONE; the Glory of Christ Jesus is manifested;
**Sinners come to Christ Jesus**
**As the incense of Praise and Worship Covers the Mercy Seat**
**And access to the Presence is opened.**

# True Worship To The Living God Comes From The Heart;
# The Tabernacle of David, Zion, Exemplified This Worship

*Unless the Lord builds the house, its builders labor in vain. (Psalm 127:1)*

Zion is the Lord's House;
The Lord is the architect and builder of Zion; David was an instrument.
The House of God is built with living stones,
Those filled with Christ, who is LIFE.
The fire of God is in Zion,
His furnace in Jerusalem (The New Jerusalem, His Bride). (Isaiah 31:9)
God infuses The Bride of Christ with His fire.
Her love for Him is as strong as death and burns like a blazing fire.
**The House of God is built with Living Stones on Fire.**

True worship is born out of the fire of God.
And comes from a consecrated heart.
It is based on an understanding of who is being worshiped.
You have to "know" God to be able to worship Him as God.
You have to "know" God to worship in His Spirit and in His Truth.
King David was a man after God's own heart.
David sought <u>one thing</u> above all else: the heart of God.
King David sought the heart of God and found Him as the Psalms attest.

David knew where he came from; watching over the sheep.
He knew that God had brought him from death to LIFE,
From shepherd to king;
That his LIFE was found in the Presence of God by the Holy Spirit within him.

God showed David, Gad and Nathan what true worship was to consist of,
And David built his Tabernacle and operated in it accordingly.
It was not elaborate, only a simple tent.
The Tabernacle of David exemplified the praise and worship that God seeks.
Because there He was worshiped in Spirit and in Truth.
That is why it is called Zion, the City of God, where the fire of God resides,
Foreshadowing the New Jerusalem that was to come;
The final and eternal City of the Living God, The Bride of Christ.

God revealed Himself to David and all Israel through His manifest Presence;

God supernaturally "kept" and prospered Israel for 36 years during David's reign.
The Tabernacle of David, was the vehicle that brought this about.
It is the prototype of God's desire for His Church today.
God was enthroned on the praises that emanated from the Tabernacle of David.
He desires to be enthroned on the praise of His Church today.
That is what it means to "lift Jesus up."
He is lifted up when we enthrone Him on our praise and worship.
He then draws all men to Himself; New Covenant evangelism.
God will "keep" and prosper His Church today
When we enthrone Him in our praise and worship from our hearts;
Then, He will "live in" the praises of His people and manifest his Presence;
Pushing back the evil, demonic authorities and powers in the heavenly realms
Giving the people of God victory wherever they are;
Creating the "open Heaven" so often spoken of, the Glory realm of God.

The Tabernacle of David was and is called Zion,
God's "Holy Hill," the City of God;
It is the Israel of God, the Church of God, the Bride of Christ, the Heart of God;
Zion comprises a people, abandoned to God, who have laid down their lives,
And become ONE with Christ Jesus and the Father,
In accordance with the prayer of Christ Jesus in John 17;
A people in complete unity; ONE with God, by the power of the Spirit of God.

## In The Last Days, In Our Day,
## God Promises To Rebuild David's Fallen Tent
*After this I will return and rebuild David's fallen tent.*
*Its ruins I will rebuild, and I will restore it,*
*That the remnant of men may seek the Lord,*
*And all the Gentiles who bear my name,*
*Says the Lord, who does these things*
*That have been known for ages. (Acts 15:16-18)*

The Tabernacle of David that had fallen down prior to The Day of Pentecost
Will be rebuilt, that the remnant of men may seek the Lord,
In the last days, in our day.
This has been a progressive restoration since the "Reformation,"
As has been all biblical truth.
The Bride of Christ in this generation will be the instrument
That God uses to rebuild The Tabernacle of David in its fullness;
The "Woman" of Revelation 12.

## Worship In Spirit And In Truth Eliminates the Veil
The Ark of the Covenant in The Tabernacle of David was not behind a veil.
There was no need for this because there was continuous worship
The worshipers were ONE with their God and there was no need for separation.
Their worship was a sweet smelling incense offered up to God
That covered the Mercy Seat.

Worship God In Spirit And In Truth

Worshiping in Spirit and in Truth protected them from the awesome holiness of God;
The same holiness that killed Uzzah when he irreverently touched the ark.

King David understood this and set up The Tabernacle of David to this end.
The Tabernacle worshipers offered God continual worship, 24 hours a day.
The Tabernacle of David is the type of worship
That God intended that we possess in the New Covenant;
That we continually worship God in Spirit and in Truth.
That we live continually in His Presence, continually in His Glory.

## On The Day Of Pentecost, And Thereafter, God Poured Out His Spirit On All Flesh

To enable us to get "in the Spirit" and out of the flesh,
So that He might meet with us individually and corporately and speak to us.
The apostle Peter declare about this day:

*In the last days* (the final two thousand years of "Time")
*I will pour out my Spirit on all people.*
*Your sons and daughters will prophesy*
(That is hear from God and speak that received to His people),
*Your young men will see visions, your old men dream dreams.*
*Even on my servants, both men and women,*
*I will pour out my Spirit in those days, and they will prophesy. (Acts 2:17-18)*

The Day of Pentecost was the beginning of a Revival that was to never end,
And it continues to this day in the hearts of those called by God.

## Christ Jesus Provides Vision For His Church

In the Old Covenant this was the pillar of cloud by day
And the pillar of fire by night.
They were baptized into Moses and the sea;
The drank from the Rock which was Christ;
They met God at The Tent of Meeting, and he spoke to them.

In the New Covenant we are led by Christ in us;
Without "vision" or "revelation" the Church of God perishes.
Prophesy, dreams and visions give the Body of Christ the "vision" they need
So that they will not perish;
Allowing the "charismatic" Christ in them to provide all necessary illumination.
The Scriptures teach that Christ Jesus is the Spirit of prophesy;
Christ in His Body provides "vision" and "revelation;"
Christ leads His Body into all Truth and tells them what is yet to come.
We eat the Bread from Heaven, Christ, the Bread of LIFE;
We drink the Water of LIFE, from Christ in us;
We live by every word that proceeds from the mouth of God;
Every word in His written Word
And every quicken word spoken in the here and now.

## Pentecost Began A Never Ending Revival

The Day of Pentecost ignited a never ending Revival;
The Father imparted His Holy Spirit to indwell His saints;
He baptized (immersed) His saints in the Holy Spirit and Fire.
They received power when this happened;
Power to live for Christ and power to do the works of Christ.
Christ Jesus said He came to bring a fire;
This fire was ignited on The Day of Pentecost
And has been burning in every generation since.
The only people who can worship in Spirit and in Truth
Are those who have received their personal Day of Pentecost.
Christ Jesus is "The Charismatic" and the "Inventor of Pentecost."
On the Day of Pentecost He gave birth to a "Charismatic people;"
He, reproduced Himself in His people, Christ in them their hope of Glory,
As the Book of acts clearly demonstrates.
Christianity, is Christ reproducing Himself in His people;
He becomes ONE with them.


## Revivals Are Times And Meetings Consecrated By God's Glory

**God** consecrated the meetings of John Westley and George Whitfield
With His Glory as they broke from the Church of England
To preach the Gospel to the common people in the open fields of the countryside.
**God** consecrated the meetings of the First Great Awakening in America.
For approximately ten years God reawakened America to the reality of His Christ;
Falling upon whole communities and regions,
Using Johnathan Edwards as one of the instruments of His Glory.
**God** consecrated the meetings of the Second Great Awakening  for many years,
As He reawakened America to the reality of His Christ;
Using Charles Finney as one of the instruments of His Glory.
**God** consecrated the meetings of Maria Etter with His Glory,
Falling on whole communities and regions, healing the worst diseases and afflictions.
**God** brought the America and the world to the Azusa Street Mission
And William Seymour in a great move of the Spirit of God, revealing His Glory.
**God** poured out His Spirit on mainline churches,
In the Charismatic Renewal, revealing His Glory.
**God** brought the world to Toronto, Canada to experience His manifest Presence;
Consecrating the meetings with His Glory.
**God** brought people from far and wide to Brownsville, Florida
To give their lives to Christ and to be baptized.

These are but a few examples of the meetings and Revivals
God has visited upon His Church, consecrated by His Glory.
He has left no nation untouched by Revival.
The out working of each of these "Revivals" continues to this day,
And all of them find their origin in The Day of Pentecost.

## Give Me No Rest And Give Yourselves No Rest
## Until Zion Is Made The Praise Of The Earth

God says to every Christian: *"Give yourselves no rest,*
*And give Me no rest, until Zion is made the praise of the earth."* (Isaiah  62)
Zion will be made the praise of the earth by the power of the Spirit of God
In those who worship God in Spirit and in Truth, in the here and now,
And bring the Kingdom of God to earth as in heaven.

## The Old Covenant And It's Ark

The Ark of the Covenant was first made to reside in The Tabernacle of Moses.
It contained the Ten Commandments on tablets of stone,
The container of manna and Aaron's rod that budded.
The Ark stood behind the veil in the Holy of Holies.
Daily, the high priest burned incense before the veil which was before the Ark.
This incense was symbolic of the worship in The Tabernacle of David.
**The worship in The Tabernacle of David**
**Allowed God to have the Ark of His Presence, unveiled;**
It allowed God to continually release His Glory and Presence.
In the Tabernacle of Moses, once a year, the high priest went behind the veil,
Without his priestly garments, barefoot,
To sprinkle the Mercy Seat with blood, to atone for the sins of the nation.
He went before the Mercy Seat, vulnerable, risking his life.
Just as with the high priest, in worship, we come before the Mercy Seat of Christ.
When we worship in Spirit and in Truth our worship is acceptable to God.
We are testifying that we filled with Christ, and living in the New Covenant
Purchased by the blood of Christ Jesus
That He, Himself, sprinkled on the Mercy Seat in Heaven for us.
Our very lives have been purchased by the blood of Christ Jesus.
Christ Jesus found us dead and has given us LIFE.
**Our worship is our response to that reality.**

## The New Covenant Ark

In the New Covenant God, takes His law out of the box, the Ark,
And puts it in the minds and writes it on the hearts of His people,
Immersing them in the Holy Spirit; saturating them in the Holy Spirit.
Again and again, forever;
Continually satisfying their never ending thirst for His Living Water.
Christ Jesus is the Bread of Heaven for those who eat of Him, continually.
Christ Jesus is the rod that budded, the "Branch" who blooms His Church.
In the New Covenant worship in Spirit and Truth removes the veil to His Presence,
And allows God to release His Presence and Glory.
When we fail to worship Him in Spirit and in Truth
He cannot release His Presence and His Glory, otherwise we would die;
If we are not in a consecrated state before Him,
And His Presence is released, we would die.
God is God of the Old and new Covenants, He never changes.

**15**

<u>Worship God In Spirit And In Truth</u>

His Presence is sacred and awesome;
No unsanctified, unconsecrated person can stand in His Presence.
At the Battle of Armageddon,
Christ Jesus defeats Satan with the Glory of His appearing; His Presence,
And the word of His mouth.

In the New Covenant the Church,
The Bride of Christ, contains His Glory; Christ in us,
But this Glory is only manifested
When she is in a sanctified, consecrated state before Him.
Jesus declared that He had given the people of God His Glory in John 17;
That is for a remnant, and it has always been a remnant, throughout the ages.
It will be true for The Bride of Christ in The Time Of The END.
It will be true for those who love God
With all their heart, soul, mind and strength;
Who have a passion for the New Covenant and the "new wine" it consists of.
Many will say the "old wine" is better
As Christ Jesus said of the Jewish religion of His day;
Many prefer a religion that has "form,"
And demands virtually nothing except rote tradition and rules made by men.
Such religion is a useless pretense, and does not have the power to save anyone.
Such religion always resists the Holy Spirit;
And hates those who are filled with the Spirit and operate in the Spirit,
As Stephen, the first martyr of the Church testified, before he was stoned to death.

## His Presence Makes A Way Where There Is No Way
The Presence of God parted the Red Sea
Allowing the Israelites to escape their enemies.
The Ark of His Presence parted the Jordan River
And allowed the Israelites to cross over into the Promised Land.
God's Presence caused the walls of Jericho to fall down.
His Presence will take The Bride of Christ, the "Woman" of Revelation 12,
Into the desert on the wings of an eagle,
Just as the children of Israel were taken into the desert on the wings of an eagle.
His Presence makes a way where there is no way.
Worship in Spirit and in Truth brings His Presence.

## Christ Jesus, Lifted Up, Draws All Men To Himself
## Hands Lifted Up To Heaven Are The Banner Of Christ Jesus
When Christ Jesus is lifted up in true worship,
When He is enthroned on the praises of His people,
He draws all men to Himself;
This is the purpose of worship and the plan of salvation;
That men get saved and live saved,
In an environment of continual worship, on earth as in Heaven.
**God intended that every Christian be a full participant**

**In this glorious enterprise.**

An Old covenant example of this involved Moses a "type" of Christ:
*The Amalekites came and attacked the Israelites at Rephidim.*
*Moses said to Joshua, 'Choose some of our men and go out to fight the Amalekites.*
*Tomorrow I will stand on top of the hill with the staff of God in my hands.'*
*So Joshua fought the Amalekites as Moses had ordered,*
*And Moses, Aaron and Hur went to the top of the hill.*
*As long as Moses held up his hands, the Israelites were winning,*
*But whenever he lowered his hands, the Amalekites were winning.*
*When Moses' hands grew tired,*
*They took a stone and put it under him and he sat on it.*
*Aaron and Hur held his hands up—one on one side, one on the other--*
*So that his hands remained steady till sunset.*
*So Joshua overcame the Amalekite army with the sword.(Exodus 17:8-13)*

*Moses built an altar and called it The Lord is my Banner.*
*He said, 'For hands were lifted up to the throne of the Lord.*
*The Lord will be at war against the Amalekites form generation to generation.'*

The power of God is released on our behalf
When we lift up our hands to the throne of the Lord in the New Covenant,
And we gain victory over our enemies (the Amalekites, a type of the godless).
Lifting hands to the Lord is worship.
It is also instructive that Moses could not do it on his own, he needed help.
In the New Covenant as we lift each other up the power of God is released.
The more of us lifting up Christ Jesus and each other the more power is released.
The Lord is our Banner and our hands uplifted to Him become His banner,
Before which His enemies and ours are defeated.

## True Worship Is Irresistible To All Who Hear God's Call
God is continually speaking to, calling, every living person.
True worship is irresistible to those who hear the call of God.
When the Body of Christ worships God in His Spirit and in His Truth,
The manifest Presence of God comes.
His Presence clears the Church and the geographical area
Of the domineering, demonic spirits that otherwise rule;
Unsaved people are released from their control and bondage,
And become free to choose Christ Jesus as their Lord and Savior;
Free to be immersed, baptized in His Spirit and set free.
True worship, sets everyone free
Free to worship their God in Spirit and in Truth.
As true worship progresses,
Whole regions and nations can be brought to Christ Jesus.
This is what is called "Revival"
That has occurred many times since the resurrection of Christ Jesus.
The Day of Pentecost was a "Revival" that was to never end and it never did end.

And all subsequent Revivals will have the characteristics of The Day of Pentecost,
Because all Revivals emanate from The Day of Pentecost and
Because Christ Jesus is "The Charismatic," "The Inventor of Pentecost."

## Worship In Spirit And In Truth
## Causes The River Of God To Flow
## And The River Of God Brings The Water Of LIFE

Christ Jesus came to give us LIFE in His Spirit.
He is LIFE, the eternal, unchangeable LIFE; the Self-Existent LIFE.
The essence of God is found in His River of LIFE.
The River of God runs through the middle of the City of God, Zion,
The Bride of Christ, the Church of God, the Israel of God.
Bringing continual LIFE to it.
The River of LIFE contains the Water of LIFE that Christ Jesus came to bring.
Christ Jesus said that those who were thirsty could come to Him
And He would give them streams of Living Water
That would flow from their innermost being.
This flow is initiated by the immersion or baptism in the Holy Spirit
Just as the 120 received on The Day of Pentecost, and all those thereafter.
We find LIFE in His Spirit when we allow Christ, the River of LIFE
To flow in and through us.
Worship in Spirit and in Truth is produced by Christ in us.
He is the Spirit and He is the Truth; He is the Water of LIFE.
We worship in Spirit and in Truth,
When we allow the Spirit to worship in and through us.
Then we experience the freedom and victory Christ Jesus came to bring;
Then He releases His Presence and Glory.
**The joy we find in this reality is our strength.**

## To Those Who Have, Even More Will Be Given

Wherever we are in God He always has more for us, forever.
Our infinite God has an infinite amount to give.
We all must have something, to be given more.
Christ Jesus begins by giving us a measure of faith in Him.
We then make a confession of that faith.
As we press into that faith He gives us more faith;
He immerses us, baptizes us in His Holy Spirit.
This is just the beginning of what can be a never ending increase.
There is an infinite supply of the Water of LIFE in the River of LIFE.
To those who have, even more will be given, forever.

When we worship God in Spirit and in Truth,
We are drinking from the River of LIFE;
The more we drink the more LIFE we have,
The more LIFE we have the more He can give to us.
**Having more is only determined by how much we want.**

For Christ Jesus, His zeal for God consumed Him.
He had food to eat that no one knew of, that came directly from His Father.
For the apostle Paul,
God did exceedingly and abundantly above what he could think or ask.
No eye has seen, no ear has heard what God has prepared for those who love Him
But He has revealed it to us by His Spirit,
And the Spirit searches all things even the deep things of God.
David asked for one thing: More of God
David knew that one day in the Presence of God was worth a thousand other days.
**One meeting in the Presence of God is worth a thousand other meetings.**
**One word spoken by God is worth a thousand words spoken by man;**
**One "quickened" word from God is priceless.**

Jesus said: *To Him who is thirsty*
*I will give to drink without cost from the spring of the water of life.*
*He who overcomes will inherit **all this**,*
*And I will be his God and he will be my son. (Revelation 21:6-7)*
**All this** is the infinite provision of the Spirit of the Living God.

## Every Work For God Must Spring From True Worship
When the people of God submit themselves to Christ Jesus
And worship their God in Spirit and in Truth
God manifests His Glory and accomplishes His plan and purposes.
Every work for God must spring from true worship,
And be infused with His Glory;
Then its yoke is easy and its burden light.
The people asked Christ Jesus what work God required of them.
He told them the work required of them was to believe in the One God sent.
If we believe, we have faith, if we have faith, we seek the face of God.
If we seek the face of God, He reveals Himself to us;
He reveals His Glory, His manifest Presence.
Then all things are possible;
Then His plan and purposes are accomplished.

## True Worship Comes From An Altar Of Uncut Stones
True worship is accomplished in us, through Christ;
We do not create it, He creates it in us.
True worship will create an altar to God untouched by the hands of man.
Often, we begin in the natural, but must allow Christ to take over.
If He does not take over, it is not true worship in Spirit and in Truth.

**Elisha needed a word from God.**
He called for the harpist
To help him get out of the natural into the supernatural.
Once in the supernatural, he received the word from God he needed.
The key to worshiping in Spirit and in Truth is to allow God to take over.
To loose our self-consciousness and become God conscious;

## Worship God In Spirit And In Truth

To get "in the Spirit;" to abandon ourselves to God.
Skill can be helpful or a hindrance depending ones willingness to let go.
If we hold too tightly to the "form" we will miss the substance.
**As has been said, We must let go and let God.**

Manifestations of uncut stone, altar worship include:
Prophetic words, words of knowledge, words of wisdom
A new song, born out of the Spirit of Christ in us;
Singing in the Spirit; dancing in the Spirit; marching in the Spirit;
Running in the Spirit; Shouting in the Spirit;
Impromptu instrumentals, involving one or more instruments, etc.
These are all expressions of the freedom Christ died to bring to His people;
Expressions of worshiping in Spirit and in Truth.

## Extravagant Worship Releases The Fragrance Of Christ

The sinful woman who came to anoint Christ Jesus is an example of true worship.
Profound gratitude compelled her to show Him extravagant worship
For the extravagant act of forgiveness and salvation He had extended to her.
She willingly expended a years wages to anoint Him with a precious perfume;
She gave to Christ Jesus all that she had to give,
Just as Christ Jesus gives us all He has to give, which is everything worth having.
This woman sets a standard for the Body of Christ.
It is a high bar.
What is LIFE worth? LIFE comprising all that Christ gives to us.
Why do we worship? Because He loves us and gives us all He has to give,
**Which is wonderful, beyond calculation; holding nothing back!**
**This woman's act of worship released a fragrance.**
**As we worship the fragrance of Christ is released,**
**And there are no limits to the extent of its influence.**

## We Do Not Struggle Against Flesh And Blood (Ephesians 6)

Our struggle is against the devil's schemes;
Against rulers, authorities and powers in this dark world
And against the spiritual forces of evil in heavenly realms.
Only the Lord, Christ in us, is able to bring victory against these adversaries.
These were the real enemies that came against King Jehoshaphat and Israel,
And through the praise of His people, the Lord brought them victory.
**The devil must stand down, stand back and depart,**
**When the people of God praise their God.**

## Put On The Full Armor Of God (Ephesians 6)

What is our part in the battle?
To be strong in the Lord and in His mighty power;
To put on all that the Lord has given us, the full armor of God:
  • The belt of Truth
  • The breastplate of righteousness

<u>Worship God In Spirit And In Truth</u>

- Readiness to proclaim the good news
- The shield of faith
- The helmet of salvation
- The sword of the Spirit

Then we are to stand in this armor and pray in the Spirit;
Worship in Spirit and in Truth.

## The Battle Belongs To The Lord

This principle is taught to us in 2 Chronicles 20.
King Jehoshaphat is told that a vast army was coming against him.
He was alarmed and determined to inquire of the Lord as to what to do.
He proclaimed a fast for the nation;
The whole nation came to Jerusalem and the temple and stood before the Lord.
King Jehoshaphat prayed to the Lord.
He declared that the Lord is the God of heaven
Who rules over all the kingdoms of the earth;
Who promised that if His people would stand in His Presence and cry out to Him,
He would hear and save His people.
King Jehoshaphat said, we do not know what do do, but our eyes are fixed upon You.

Then the Spirit of the Lord came upon one of the Levities,
And he prophesied, do not be discouraged
Because the battle belongs to the Lord.
The Lord instructed the people to march out against the enemy,
Telling them that they would not have to fight.
Then some of the Levities stood and praised the Lord, the God of Israel
With a very loud voice.

The next morning King Jehoshaphat stood before the people and told them
To have faith in the Lord and His prophets and they would be successful.
After consulting with the people, he appointed men to sing to the Lord
And to praise Him for the splendor of his holiness;
They went out at the head of the army, singing:
"Give thanks to the Lord, for His love endures forever."
As they began to sing and praise, the Lord set ambushes against the enemy,
And they were completely defeated.
**The Lord rose up on the praises of His people and destroyed the enemy.**
**The Lord will rise up on our praises today and give us victory.**

## The Kingdom Of God Advances Forcefully
## And Forceful Men Lay Hold Of It

*From the days of John the Baptist until now, the kingdom of heaven*
*Has been forcefully advancing, and forceful men lay hold of it. (Matthew 11:12)*

Jehoash king of Israel came to see Elisha who was dying:
*Elisha said, 'Get a bow and some arrows,' and he did so .*

*'Take the bow in your hands,' he said to the king of Israel.*
*When he had taken it, Elisha put his hands on the king's hands.*

*'Open the east window,' he said, and he opened it.*
*'Shoot!' Elisha said, and he shot.*
*'The Lord's arrow of victory, the arrow of victory over Aram!'*
*Elisha declared. 'You will completely destroy the Arameans at Aphek.'*

*Then he said, 'Take the arrows,' and the king took them .*
*Elisha told him, 'Strike the ground,'*
*He struck it three times and stopped.*
*The man of God was angry with him and said,*
*'You should have struck the ground five or six times,*
*Then you would have defeated Aram and completely destroyed it.*
*But now you will defeat it only three times.'*

**What Elisha told king Jehoash is a worship principle.**
If we want victory in our worship we must persist into His Presence
And through His Presence to complete victory.
We must not stop before we have complete victory.
We must stop only when the Spirit releases us to stop.

God desires that we achieve victory over our enemy in our worship;
He has provide the means for us to do this by His Presence.
However, if we do not press in forcefully, until our enemy is destroyed,
We will have only a partial victory at best.
We cannot content ourselves with partial victories;
Our enemy does not.
He wants to see us completely destroyed and eternally dead.
This is similar to the concept of "praying through."
We can "pray through" until God lets us know we have victory in our prayer.
Likewise in praise and worship we can persist until we know we have the victory;
Heaven is opened and the enemy defeated.
In fact our persistence can create a continuous open Heaven.

**Jacob wrestled with God until he was blessed:**
*So Jacob was left alone, and a man wrestled with him till daybreak.*
*When the man saw that he could not overpower him,*
*He touched the socket of Jacob's hip so that his hip was wrenched*
*As he wrestled with the man.*
*Then the man said, 'Let me go, for it is daybreak.'*
*But Jacob replied, 'I will not let you go unless you bless me.'*
*The man asked him, 'What is your name?'*
*'Jacob,' he answered.*
*Then the man said, 'Your name will no longer be Jacob, but Israel,*
*Because you have struggled with God and with men and have overcome.'*
*Jacob said, 'Please tell me your name.'*

<u>Worship God In Spirit And In Truth</u>

*But he replied, "Why do you ask my name.'*
*Then he blessed him there.*
*So Jacob call the place Peniel, saying,*
*'It is because I saw God face to face, and yet my life was spared.(Genesis32:24-32)*

Jacob knew it was crucial to his life that he receive the blessing of God,
And he was not going to let go of God until he was blessed.
This needs to be the attitude of our worship.
We must not let go of God until He manifests His Presence;
Until we see Him face to face; until we are blessed.

## Worship Brings The Baptism In The Holy Spirit
After the resurrection of Christ Jesus He told His disciples:

*'Do not leave Jerusalem, but wait for the gift my Father promised,*
*Which you have heard me speak about.*
*For John baptized with water,*
*But in a few days you will be baptized with the Holy Spirit. (Acts 1:4-5)*

*Then they (the disciples) returned to Jerusalem*
*From the Hill called the Mount of Olives,*
*A Sabbath day's walk from the city.*
*When they arrived,*
*They went upstairs to the room where they were staying.*
*Those present were Peter, John, James and Andrew; Philip and Thomas,*
*Bartholomew and Mathew; James son of Alphaeus and Simon the Zealot,*
*And Judas son of James.*
***They all joined together constantly in prayer,***
*Along with the women and Mary the mother of Jesus, and his brothers.*
*(Acts1:12-14)*

*When the day of Pentecost came, they were all together in one place.*
*Suddenly a sound like the blowing of a violent wind came from heaven*
*And filled the whole house where they were sitting.*
*They saw what seemed to be tongues of fire that separated*
*And came to rest on each of them.*
*All of them were filled with the Holy Spirit*
*And began to speak in other tongues as the Spirit enabled them. (Acts 2:1-4)*

## Worship Sets The Captives Free
Paul and Silas had been arrested and beaten and thrown in prison:
*About midnight Paul and Silas were praying and singing hymns to God,*
*And the other prisoners were listening to them.*
*Suddenly there was such a violent earthquake*
*That the foundations of the prison were shaken.*
*At once all the prison doors flew open, and everybody's chains came loose.*
*The jailer woke up, and when he saw the prison door open,*

<u>Worship God In Spirit And In Truth</u>

*He drew his sword and was about to kill himself*
*Because he thought the prisoners had escaped.*
*But Paul shouted, 'Don't harm yourself! We are all here!'*
*The jailer called for lights, rushed in and fell trembling before Paul and Silas.*
*He then brought them out and asked, 'Sirs, what must I do to be saved?'*

*They replied, 'Believe in the Lord Jesus, and you will be saved—*
*You and your household.'*

Here the worship of Paul and Silas, their praying and singing,
Brought the Presence of God in a mighty way.
This is how God responds to those who consecrate themselves to God
And worship Him; miracles occur!


## <u>Praise Until The Spirit Of Worship Comes,</u>
## <u>Worship Until The Glory Falls;</u>
## <u>Then Experience Intimacy With Christ Jesus</u>
This was the admonishment and attitude of Ruth Ward Heflin,
And came from her life long pursuit of God and her experience in God.
We can begin to praise God in the natural;
This enables us to get "in the Spirit."
Once we are "in the Spirit" we can worship Him until He releases His Glory,
His manifest Presence.
Then, we can enjoy intimacy with the love of our LIFE, Christ Jesus,
For as long as we desire.
**This intimacy was the intoxication of The Day of Pentecost.**
Once you have experienced this intimacy you will never be the same again;
You will know why David asked for "one thing" above all else.
One hour in this intimacy is worth a thousand hours
Experiencing what ever is second best.
You will never want to leave this intimacy; it is Heaven on earth.
**For the rest of your life**
**You will desire this intimacy with Christ Jesus above all else;**
**Nothing else will satisfy you; you are spoiled for life,**
Which is exactly what God wants to do for you.
The only thing standing in your way is your willingness to enter in.
**Christ Jesus is waiting for you!**


## <u>The Song Of Songs Teaches Us The Intimacy Of Worship</u>
The following are paraphrases out of the Song of Songs put into poetic form;
It is The Bride of Christ speaking to her Lover, Christ Jesus
And Christ Jesus speaking to His Bride.

**The Bride of Christ Speaking To Christ Jesus:**
I belong to you my King
My desire is for you alone
Place me like a seal over your heart
Like a brand upon your arm
For my love for you is as strong as death
It burns like a blazing fire
An ocean of water cannot quench my love
A river cannot wash it away

All the wealth of this world
Is as nothing compared to our love.
Every delicacy both new and old
I have stored up for you my love
For my love for you is as strong as death
It burns like a blazing fire
An ocean of water cannot quench my love
A river cannot wash it away

Come away with me my lover my friend
Let me be your complete contentment

Let me be your complete contentment

**Christ Jesus Speaking To His Bride:**
Who is this that appears like the dawn
Fair as the moon Bright as the sun
Majestic as the stars all beautiful you are
There is no flaw in you

You have stolen my heart my sister my bride
With one glance of your eyes

How delightful is your love my darling
Better than wine, fragrant as perfume
You are a garden fountain, a well of flowing water
There is no one like you

You have stolen my heart my sister my bride
With one glance of your eyes

The King is captivated by your beauty
The King is captivated by you.

## True Worship Creates Unity In The Body Of Christ
## Unity In Worship Commands The Blessing Of God
True worship and praise to God creates "Oneness" with God as nothing else can,
And "Oneness" with God creates unity in the Body of Christ.
In Heaven, all are ONE, and therefore they praise and worship the Living God.
On earth, when we worship in Spirit and in Truth, God makes us ONE,
By the power of His Spirit;
We are transformed by the words of our mouth, by Christ in us,
And He brings the unity in His Body He desires.
Unity in worship commands the blessing of God.

*Behold how good and how pleasant it is for brethren to dwell together in unity!*
*It is like the precious ointment poured on the head, that ran down on the beard,*
*Even the beard of Aaron [the first high priest],*
*That came down upon the collar and skirts of his garments*
*[Consecrating the whole body]; [Exodus 30:25,30]*
*Like the dew of [lofty] Mount Hermon,*
*And the dew that comes on the Hills of Zion;*
*For there the Lord has commanded the blessing,*
*Even life forevermore [upon the high and lowly]. (Psalm 133, Amplified)*

## The Worship of Every Saint Matters And Makes a Difference
We are "living stones" built into The New Jerusalem, The City of God,
Who's architect and builder is God.
The worship of every saint adds to the whole, a living, necessary part,
And adds to the power of God released.
In worship every single saint makes a difference.
Every heart set on Christ makes a difference.
Every voice makes a difference.
Every pair of hands lifted up makes a difference.
Everyone dancing makes a difference.
Every act of worship makes a difference.
There are no insignificant acts of worship before the Living God.

## The Remnant Who Turns Back The Battle At The Gate

In The Time of The END, The Bride of Christ will turn back the battle at the gate.

*In that day* the Lord Almighty
*Will be a glorious crown, a beautiful wreath*
*For the remnant of His people.*
*He will be a Spirit of justice to Him* (Christ) *who sits in judgment,*
*A source of strength to those* (The Bride of Christ)
*Who turn back the battle at the gate. (Isaiah 28:5-6)*

We have learned that the battle belongs to the Lord,
But we are His instruments of battle
As we enthrone Him in our praise and worship.
**Lord make us instruments for Your Glory!**

## The Bride Of Christ
## Will Bear The Ark Of The Presence
## On Her Shoulders

When David became king
He realized that that Israel had not been inquiring of the Ark of the Presence
Since it had been captured by the Philistines, at the defeat of Saul.
However, the Philistines had returned it, because of the havoc it cause among them,
And it wound up at the house of Abinadab.
David went to the house of Abinadab and placed the Ark on a new cart,
And proceeded to bring it back to Jerusalem.
Along the way an oxen stumbled,
And one of David's soldiers, Uzzah, reached out his hand to steady the Ark.
This irreverence angered the Lord
And He struck Uzzah dead because he had put his hand on the Ark.

This caused David to be angry and to fear the Lord,
And he asked, *'How can I ever bring the ark of God to me.' (1 Chronicles 13:12)*
Not wanting to take the Ark any further he took it to the house of Obed-Edom,
Where it remained for three months.
During this time the Ark of the Presence blessed Obed-Edom's household
In everything that they did.

David then realized that he had taken the wrong approach in transporting the Ark.
He realized that it was to be borne on the shoulders of Levites alone,
As the Lord had instructed Moses.
David said: *'It was because you, the Levites, did not bring it up the first time*
*That the Lord our God broke out in anger against us.*
*We did not inquire of him about how to do it in the prescribed way.'*
*So the priests and the Levites consecrated themselves*
*In order to bring up the ark of the Lord, the God of Israel.*
*And the Levites carried the ark of God with the poles on their shoulders,*

**27**

Worship God In Spirit And In Truth

*As Moses had commanded in accordance with the world of the Lord.*

*David told the leaders of the Levites*
*To appoint their brothers as singers to sing joyful songs,*
*Accompanied by musical instruments; lyres, harps and cymbals.*
*(1 Chronicles 15:13-16)*

*So David and the elders of Israel and the commanders of units of a thousand*
*Went to bring up the ark of the covenant of the Lord*
*From the house of Obed-Edom, with rejoicing. (1 Chronicles 15:25)*

*So all Israel brought up the ark of the covenant of the Lord with shouts,*
*With the sounding of rams' horns and trumpets, and of cymbals,*
*And the playing of lyres and harps. (1 Chronicles 15:28)*

**Today**, we as the priests of God, must consecrate ourselves before God
That we might bear the Ark of His Presence
With the same reverence and the same joyfulness
As did King David, the Levites and all Israel.
The Ark of His Presence is to be borne on our shoulders,
By our will, consecration and obedience
To it's place of highest honor,
Enthroned on the heartfelt praise and worship of our King, Jesus.

Without the Ark of His Presence,
Israel was no different than any other nation of that time.
Today without the manifest Presence of God
We are no different than any other people.
The manifest Presence of God is a matter of life and death for His Church.
The Bride of Christ will understand this.
She will carry the Presence of God on Her shoulders,
Enthroning Christ Jesus on Her extravagant praise and worship.

## A Glimpse Of Heaven Inspired Praise

*Praise the Lord*
*Praise God in his sanctuary;*
*Praise him for his acts of power;*
*Praise him for his surpassing greatness.*
*Praise him with the sounding trumpet,*
*Praise him with the harp and lyre,*
*Praise him with tambourine and dancing,*
*Praise him with the strings and flute,*
*Praise him with resounding cymbals.*
*Let everything that has breath praise the lord*
*Praise the Lord. (Psalm 150)*

Worship God In Spirit And In Truth

## The Psalms Are Our Teacher
Many of the Psalms were born out of the Tabernacle of David;
Out of Zion, The City of God, where the fire of God resides.
The Psalms are our teacher.
They teach us the nature and character of Heavenly praise and worship;
Praise and worship that brings the Kingdom of God to earth as in Heaven.

## Your Kingdom Come, Your Will Be Done,
## On Earth As In Heaven
This is the heart cry of The Bride of Christ;
This is the object of Her unquenchable zeal;
This is what happens when the people of God worship their God
In Spirit and in Truth.
This is what happened on that "Holy Hill," Zion, in The Tabernacle of David;
This is the foreshadow of The New Jerusalem, the eternal dwelling of God.

Christ Jesus intends for us to live continuously in His Presence.
When we worship God in Spirit and in Truth
We can live continuously in His Presence and His manifest Glory.
Then there is continuous victory over our enemies;
Then the plan and purpose for our lives and His Church is made complete.
This is where Christ Jesus is leading us at this time.
He is going to bring about the answer to His own prayer (John 17)
**And make us ONE with Himself.**

**Shake off the spirit of religion that is only empty form,**

**Abandon yourself to God and see what He will do through you;**

**Exceedingly and abundantly above what you can think of ask**

**By His power at work in you!**

**Christ in you the hope of glory!**

**Hallelujah!**

# The Whole World Is Under The Control Of The Devil
This reality was made clear when the devil came to test Jesus in the desert:

*Again, the devil took him to a very high mountain*
*And showed him all the kingdoms of the world and their splendor.*
*'All this I will give you,' he said, 'if you will bow down and worship me.'*
*(Matthew 4:8-9)*

*We know that we are the children of God,*
*And that the whole world is under the control of the evil one. (1 John 5:19)*

*Do not love the world or anything in the world.*
*If anyone loves the world, the love of the Father is not in him.*
*For everything in the world—the cravings of sinful man,*
*The lust of his eyes and the boasting of what he has and does--*
*Comes not from the Father but from the world.*
*The world and its desires pass away,*
*But the man who does the will of God lives forever. (1 John 2:15-17)*

It is by the grace of God the world has not destroyed itself by now.
The only reason it has not is the presence of the Holy Spirit in the people of God.
When the Holy Spirit is finally taken out of the world,
The world rushes to it's self destruction.

The only person who can stand up against the wiles of the devil is Christ Jesus;
The only way we can stand against the wiles of the devil is through Christ in us;
Through our submission to His will and His way.
The only entity that stands in the way of the devil's complete domination
Is the Church of God; those with Christ in them.
Therefore, the Church of God is the focus of the devil's deception.
If he can destroy the Church of God he has won the fight.
However, Jesus came to destroy the devil's work,
And he does so through the people he lives in,
Those who have received Christ Jesus
And have laid down their lives and received His life;
Those who have consecrated their lives to serve and worship Him.
Christ Jesus has won the victory, but we must stand with Him in that victory.

Praise and worship are the primary tools that we, the instruments of Christ Jesus,
Can use to destroy the devil's work.

# The Devil Seeks Worship
The devil seeks those who will worship him in his spirit, deceived by his lie.
He seeks those who will worship him in his spirit,
And embrace his lie, which he puts forward as the truth,
Pretending to  be an angel of light;
That each person can be like God, doing as they please, ignoring the God of Heaven.

**30**

It is also notable that he receives what he seeks;
In terms of numbers, exceedingly more than does the God of Heaven.
The people of this world give to the god of this world, whole heartedly
The worship and glory that he wants.
Virtually all that goes on in the current culture, ie.: television, movies, politics,
Social events, rock concerts, sporting events, etc., are testimonies to this fact.
The people of this world are abandon to their god,
And this abandonment leads to eternal death.
The glory of the god of this world,
Is the willingness of most of humanity to follow him to their eternal death.
The world controlled by the devil puts on a show, a pretense, like a movie prop;
When you look behind it, it is empty, without substance, without life;
The devil is the puppeteer, pulling the stings of a world he has deceived;
A world lost and destined for hell.

## True Worship Stops The Expansion of Hell
True worship mitigates, arrests and stops the enlargement of the mouth of hell,
And the eternal carnage that the worship of the devil brings,
Worship of the True and Living God in His Spirit and in His Truth,
Brings Him the Glory that is due to Him,
And brings His Presence that destroys the works of the enemy.
This worship brings about the God consciousness that causes men to turn to Him.
**All other endeavors for God must begin here.**
Abandonment to the God of Heaven leads to eternal LIFE.
God gains glory when individuals and His Church abandon themselves to Him.
This is the destiny of The Bride of Christ;
Her love for Christ Jesus is as strong as death,
And burns like a blazing fire; Forever!
**He brought Her from death to LIFE and She will never forget that!**


Know this my son you can only serve one
The prince of dark or the Prince of Light
Everyday, in all you do and say
You choose the Light or you choose the dark

There's only one Light, the Lord Jesus Christ
He is the Light in this dark world.

Turn to Him son, His victory is won
Turn away from strife, Give Jesus your life

# Worship Excerpts
# From The Old Testament

## 2 Kings
*When the Lord made a covenant with the Israelites he commanded them:*
*'Do not worship any other gods or bow down to them,*
*Serve them or sacrifice to them.*
*But the Lord, who brought you out of Egypt*
*With a mighty power and outstretched arm, is the one you must worship.*
*To him you shall bow down and to him offer sacrifices.*
*You must always be careful to keep the decrees and ordinances,*
*The laws and commands he wrote for you.*
*Do not worship other gods.*
*Do not forget the covenant I have made with you, and do not worship other gods.*
***Rather, worship the Lord your God;***
***It is he who will deliver you from the hand of all your enemies.'***
*(2 Kings 35-39)*

## David Sets Up The Tabernacle Of David
*They brought the ark of God and set it inside the tent that David had pitched for it,*
*And they presented burnt offerings and fellowship offerings before God.*
*After David had finished sacrificing the burnt offerings and fellowship offerings,*
*He blessed the people in the name of the Lord.*
*Then he gave a loaf of bread, a cake of dates and a cake of raisins*
*To each Israelite man and woman.*

*He appointed some of the Levities to minister before the ark of the Lord,*
*To make petition, to give thanks, and to praise the Lord, the God of Israel:*
*Asaph was the chief, Zechariah second,*
*Then Jeiel, Shemiramoth, Jeheil, Mattithiah, Eliab, Benaiah, Obed-Edom and Jeiel.*
*They were to play the lyers and harps, Asaph was to sound the cymbals,*
*And Benaiah and Jahaziel the priests were to blow the trumpets regularly*
*Before the ark of the covenant of God. (1 Chronicles 16:1-6)*

In The Tabernacle of David the Levites ministered before the Ark of His Presence;
The Ark was the focus of their worship
And their worship was a sweet smelling incense that covered the Mercy Seat
And brought the manifestation of His Presence.
We minister through Christ in us, in His Spirit and in His Truth
And our worship is a sweet smelling incense
That covers the Mercy Seat in Heaven,
And compels Christ to manifests His Presence.

## David's Psalm Of Thanks

That day David first committed to Asaph and his associates
This psalm of thanks to the Lord:

*Give thanks to the Lord, call on his name;*
*Make known among the nations what he has done.*
*Sing to him, sing praise to him;*
*Tell of all his wonderful acts.*
*Glory in his holy name;*
*Let the hearts of those who seek the Lord rejoice.*
*Look to the Lord and his strength; seek his face always.*
*Remember the wonders he has done, his miracles,*
*And the judgments he pronounced*
*O descendants of Israel his servant,*
*O sons of Jacob, his chosen ones.*

*He is the Lord our God; his judgments are in all the earth.*
*He remembers his covenant forever,*
*The word he commanded, for a thousand generations,*
*The covenant he made with Abraham, the oath he swore to Isaac.*
*He confirmed it to Jacob as a decree, to Israel as an everlasting covenant:*
*'To you I will give the land of Canaan as the portion you will inherit.'*

*When they were but few in number, few indeed, and strangers in it,*
*They wandered from nation to nation, from one kingdom to another.*
*He allowed no man to oppress them; for their sake he rebuked kings:*
*Do not touch my anointed ones; do my prophets no harm.*

*Sing to the Lord, all the earth;*
*Proclaim his salvation day after day.*
*Declare his glory among the nations,*
*His marvelous deeds among all peoples.*
*For great is the Lord and most worthy of praise;*
*He is to be feared above all gods.*
*For all the gods of the nations are idols,*
*But the Lord made the heavens.*
*Splendor and majesty are before him;*
*Strength and joy in his dwelling place.*
*Ascribe to the Lord glory and strength,*
*Ascribe to the Lord the glory due his name.*
*Bring an offering and come before him;*
***Worship the Lord in the splendor of his holiness.***
*Tremble before him, all the earth!*
*The world is firmly established;*
*It cannot be moved.*

*Let the heavens rejoice, let the earth be glad;*

Worship God In Spirit And In Truth

*Let them say among the nations, 'The Lord reigns!'*
*Let the sea resound, and all that is in it;*
*Let the fields be jubilant, and everything in them!*
*Then the trees of the forest will sing,*
*They will sing for joy before the Lord,*
*For he comes to judge the earth*

*Give thanks to the Lord, for he is good;*
*His love endures forever.*
***Cry out, 'save us, O God our Savior;***
*Gather us and deliver us from the nations,*
*That we may give thanks to your holy name,*
*That we may glory in your praise.'*
*Praise be to the Lord, the God of Israel,*
*From everlasting to everlasting.*

*Then all the people said 'Amen" and 'Praise the Lord.' (1 Chronicles 16:7-36)*

## Psalm 3

*But you are a shield around me, O Lord*
*My Glorious One, who lifts up my head.*
***To the Lord I cry aloud,*** *and he answers me from his holy hill* (Zion).

**Today**, are we crying out to the Lord as if our very lives depended upon it?
In reality there is no room for passivity in our Christian walk:
*From the days of John the Baptist until now,*
*The kingdom of heaven has been forcefully advancing,*
*And forceful men lay hold of it. (Matthew 11:12)*

## Psalm 5

*But let all who take refuge in you be glad;*
***Let them ever sing for joy.***
*Spread your protection over them,*
*That those who love your name may rejoice in you.*
*For surely, O Lord, you bless the righteous;*
*You surround them with your favor as with a shield. (Psalm 5:11-12)*

## Psalm 7

*I will give thanks to the Lord because of his righteousness*
*And will sing praise to the name of the Lord Most High. (Psalm 7:17)*

## Psalm 8

*From the lips of children and infants you have ordained praise*
*Because of your enemies,* ***to silence the foe and the avenger****. (Psalm 7:2)*

## Psalm 9

*I will praise you, O Lord, with all my heart;*
*I will be glad and rejoice in you;*
*I will sing praise to your name, O Most High. (Psalm 9:1-2)*

*Sing praises to the Lord, enthroned in Zion;*
*Proclaim among the nations what he has done. (Psalm 9:11)*

## Psalm 13

*But I trust in your unfailing love;*
*My heart rejoices in your salvation.*
*I will sing to the Lord, for he has been good to me. (Psalm 13:5-6)*

## Psalm 16

*I will praise the Lord, who counsels me;*
*Even at night my heart instructs me.*
*I have set the Lord always before me.*
*Because he is at my right hand, I will not be shaken.*
*Therefore my heart is glad and my tongue rejoices;*
*My body also will rest secure,*
*Because you will not abandon me to the grave,*
*Nor will you let your Holy One see decay.*
*You have made known to me the path of life;*
***You will fill me with joy in your presence,***
*With eternal pleasures at your right hand. (Psalm 16:7-11)*

It is the Presence of the Lord that brings joy, and joy strength.

## Psalm 18

*The Lord lives! Praise be to my Rock!*
*Exalted be God my Savior!*

*Therefore I will praise you among the nations, O Lord;*
*I will sing praises to your name. (Psalm 18:49)*

## Psalm 19

*May the words of my mouth and the meditation of my heart*
*Be pleasing in your sight, O Lord, my Rock and my Redeemer. (Psalm 19:14)*

## Psalm 20

*We will shout for joy when you are victorious*
*And will lift up our banners in the name of our God. (Psalm 20:5)*

## Psalm 21
*Be exalted, O Lord, in your strength;*
*We will sing and praise your might. (Psalm 21:13)*

## Psalm 22
*I will declare your name to my brothers;*
*In the congregation I will praise you.*
*You who fear the Lord, praise him! (Psalm 22:22)*

*From you comes my praise in the great assembly;*
*Before those who fear you will I fulfill my vows.*
*The poor will eat and be satisfied;*
*They who seek the Lord will praise him—*
*May your hearts live forever! (Psalm 22:25-26)*

The only ones who find the Lord
Are those who seek him continually, as David did.
We find the Lord in our worship when he manifests His Presence.

## Psalm 26
*Vindicate me, O Lord, for I have led a blameless life;*
*I have trusted in the Lord without wavering.*
*Test me, O lord, and try me, examine my heart and my mind;*
*For your love is ever before me,*
*And I walk continually in your truth.*
*I do not sit with deceitful men, nor do I consort with hypocrites;*
*I abhor the assembly of evildoers*
*And refuse to sit with the wicked.*
*I wash my hands in innocence,*
*And go about your altar, O Lord,*
***Proclaiming aloud your praise and telling of all your deeds.***
*I love the house where you live, O Lord,*
*The Place where your glory dwells.*
*Do not take away my soul along with sinners*
*Or my life with bloodthirsty men,*
*In whose hands are wicked schemes, whose hand are full of bribes.*
*But I lead a blameless life;*
*Redeem me and be merciful to me.*
*My feet stand on level ground,*
***In the great assembly I will praise the Lord.***

## Psalm 27
*At His tabernacle will I sacrifice with shouts of joy;*
*I will sing and make music to the Lord. (Psalm 27:6)*

## Psalm 28
*Hear my cry for mercy as I call to you for help,*
*As I lift up my hands toward your Most Holy Place. (Psalm 28:2)*

## Psalm 29
*And in his temple all cry, 'Glory!' (Psalm 29:9)*

## Psalm 30
*Sing to the Lord, you saints of his;*
*Praise his holy name. (Psalm 30:4)*

*You turned my wailing into dancing;*
*You removed my sackcloth and clothed me with joy,*
*That my heart may sing to you and not be silent.*
*O Lord my God, I will give you thanks forever. (Psalm 30:11-12)*

## Psalm 31
*How great is your goodness*
*Which you have stored up for those who fear you*
***In the shelter of your presence***
*You hide them from the intrigues of men;*
*In your dwelling you keep them safe from the strife of tongues. (Psalm 30:19-20)*

The Presence of the Lord is our shelter, and praise brings His Presence.

*Praise be to the Lord, for he showed his wonderful love to me*
*When I was in a besieged city. (Psalm 31:21)*

## Psalm 32
*Therefore let everyone who is godly pray to you while you may be found;*
*Surely when the mighty waters rise, they will not reach him.*
***You are my hiding place****; you will protect me from trouble*
*And surround me with songs of deliverance. (Psalm 32:6-7)*

*Rejoice in the Lord and be glad, you righteous;*
*Sing, all you who are upright in heart! )Psalm 32:11)*

## Psalm 33
*Sing joyfully to the Lord, you righteous;*
*It is fitting for the upright to praise him.*
*Praise the Lord with the harp;*
*Make music to him on the ten-stringed lyre.*
*Sing to him a new song;*
*Play skillfully, and shout for joy. (Psalm 33:1-3)*

## Psalm 34
*I will extol the Lord at all times;*
*His praise will always be on my lips.*
*My soul will boast in the Lord;*
*Let the afflicted hear and rejoice.*
*Glorify the Lord with me;*
*Let us exalt his name together. (Psalm 34:1-3)*

## Psalm 35
*I will give you thanks in the great assembly;*
*Among throngs of people I will praise you. (Psalm 35:18)*

*May those who delight in my vindication shout for joy and gladness;*
*May they always say,*
*'The Lord be exalted, who delights in the well-being of his servant.'*
*My tongue will speak of your righteousness*
*And of your praises all day long. (Psalm 35:27-28)*

## Psalm 36
*Your love, O Lord, reaches to the heavens,*
*Your faithfulness to the skies.*
*Your righteousness is like the mighty mountains,*
*Your justice like the great deep.*
*O Lord, you preserve both man and beast.*
*How priceless is your unfailing love!*
*Both high and low among men find refuge in the shadow of your house;*
***You give them drink form your river of delights.***
*For with you is the fountain of life;*
*In your light we see light. (Psalm 36:5-9)*

The drink from the "river of delights" is what the 120 experienced
On The Day of Pentecost.

## Psalm 37
*Delight yourself in the Lord and he will give you the desires of your heart.*
*(Psalm 37:4)*

## Psalm 41
*Praise be to the Lord, the God of Israel, from everlasting to everlasting.*
*(Psalm 41:13)*

## Psalm 42
*As the deer pants for streams of water, so my soul pants for you, O God.*
*My soul thirsts for God, for the living God.*
*Where can I go and meet with God? (Psalm 42:1-2)*

***Deep calls to deep*** *in the roar of your waterfalls;*
*All your waves and breakers have swept over me.*
*By day the Lord directs his love, at night his song is with me--*
*A prayer to the God of my life. (Psalm 42:7-8)*

## Psalm 43
*Then will I go to the altar of God, to God, my joy and my delight.*
*I will praise you with the harp, O God, my God. (Psalm 43:4)*

## Psalm 44
*In God we make our boast all day long,*
*And we will praise your name forever. (Psalm 44:8)*

## Psalm 45
*Daughters of kings are among your honored women;*
*At you right hand is the royal bride* (The Bride of Christ) *in gold of Ophir.*

*Listen, O daughter* (The Bride of Christ), *consider and give ear:*
*Forget your people and your father's house.*
*The king is enthralled by your beauty;*
*Honor him, for he is your Lord. (Psalm 45:9-11)*

*All glorious is the princess* (The Bride of Christ) *within her chamber;*
*Her gown is interwoven with gold.*
*In embroidered garments she is led to the king;*
*Her virgin companions follow her and are brought to you.*
*The are led in with joy and gladness;*
*They enter the palace of the King.*

*Your sons will take the place of your fathers;*
*You will make them princes throughout the land.*
*I will perpetuate your memory through all generations;*
*Therefore the nations will praise you for ever and ever. (Psalm 45:13-17)*

**This is God speaking about The Bride of Christ.**

## Psalm 46
*There is a river whose streams make glad the city of God,*
*The holy place where the Most High dwells*
*God is within her, she will not fall;*
*God will help her at break of day. (Psalm 46:4-5)*

This river is the River of God that runs from the Throne of God,
Through the middle of the City of God, The Bride of Christ.

Worship God In Spirit And In Truth

## Psalm 47
*Clap your hands, all you nations;*
*Shout to God with cries of joy.*
*How awesome is the Lord Most High,*
*The great King over all the earth!*
*He subdued nations under us, peoples under our feet.*
*He chose our inheritance for us,*
*The pride of Jacob, whom he loved.*

*God has ascended amid shouts of joy,*
*The Lord amid the sounding of trumpets.*
*Sing praises to God, sing praises;*
*Sing praises to our King, sing praises.*

*For God is the King of all the earth;*
*Sing to him a psalm of praise.*
*God reigns over the nations;*
*God is seated on his holy throne.*
*The nobles of the nations assemble*
*As the people of the God of Abraham,*
*For the kings of the earth belong to God;*
*He is greatly exalted.*

## Psalm 48
*Great is the Lord, and most worthy of praise,*
*In the city of our God, his holy mountain.*
*It is beautiful in its loftiness, the joy of the whole earth.*
*Like the utmost heights of Zaphon is Mount Zion,*
*The city of the Great King.*
*God is in her citadels;*
*He has shown himself to be her fortress. (Psalm 48:1-3)*

*Like your name, O God,*
*Your praise reaches to the ends of the earth;*
*Your right hand is filled with righteousness.*
*Mount Zion rejoices,*
*The villages of Judah are glad because of your judgments. (Psalm 48:10-11)*

## Psalm 52
*I will praise you forever for what you have done;*
*In your name I will hope, for your name is good.*
*I will praise you in the presence of your saints. (Psalm 52:9)*

## Psalm 54
*I will sacrifice a freewill offering to you;*
*I will praise your name, O Lord, for it is good.*

*For he has delivered me from all my troubles,*
*And my eyes have looked in triumph on my foes. (Psalm 54:6-7)*

## Psalm 56
*Then my enemies will turn back when I call for help.*
***By this I will know that God is for me.***
*In God, whose word I praise, in the Lord, whose word I praise--*
*In God I trust; I will not be afraid.*
*What can man do to me? (Psalm 56:9-11)*

## Psalm 57
*Be exalted, O God, above the heavens;*
*Let your glory be over all the earth. (Psalm 57:5)*

*I will praise you, O Lord, among the nations;*
*I will sing of you among the peoples*
*For great is your love, reaching to the heavens;*
*Your faithfulness reaches to the skies.*

*Be exalted, O God, above the heavens;*
*Let your glory be over all the earth. (Psalm 57:9-11)*

## Psalm 59
*But I will sing of your strength, in the morning I will sing of your love;*
*For you are my fortress, my refuge in times of trouble.*
*O my Strength, I sing praise to you;*
*You, O God, are my fortress, my loving God. (Psalm 59:16-17)*

## Psalm 61
*Then will I ever sing praise to your name*
*And fulfill my vows day after day. (Psalm 61:8)*

## Psalm 63
*O God, you are my God, earnestly I seek you;*
*My soul thirsts for you, my body longs for you,*
*In a dry and weary land where there is no water.*

*I have seen you in the sanctuary and beheld your power and your glory*
*Because your love is better than life, my lips will glorify you.*
*I will praise you as long as I live,*
*And in your name I will lift up my hands.*
*My soul will be satisfied as with the richest of foods;*
*With singing lips my mouth will praise you.*

*On my bed I remember you;*
*I think of you through the watches of the night.*

*Because you are my help,*
*I will sing in the shadow of your wings.*
*I stay close to you; your right hand upholds me.*

*They who seek my life will be destroyed;*
*They will go down to the depths of the earth.*
*They will be given over to the sword and become food for jackals.*
*But the king will rejoice in God;*
*All who swear by God's name will praise him,*
*While the mouths of liars will be silenced.*

## Psalm 64
*Let the righteous rejoice in the Lord and take refuge in him;*
*Let all the upright in heart praise him! (Psalm 64:10)*

## Psalm 65
*Praise awaits you, O God, in Zion;*
*To you our vows will be fulfilled. (Psalm 65:1)*

*Those living far away fear your wonders;*
*Where morning dawns and evening fades*
*You call forth songs of joy. (Psalm 65:8)*

*The meadows are covered with flocks and the valleys are mantled with grain;*
*They shout for joy and sing. (Psalm 65:13)*

## Psalm 66
*Shout with joy to God, all the earth!*
*Sing to the glory of his name;*
*Offer him glory and praise!*
*Say to God, 'How awesome are your deeds!*
*So great is your power that your enemies cringe before you;*
*They sing praise to you, they sing praise to your name.'*

*Come and see what God has done, how awesome his works in man's behalf!*
*He turned the sea into dry land, they passed through the river on foot--*
*Come, let us rejoice in him.*
*He rules forever by his power, his eyes watch the nations--*
*Let not the rebellious rise up against him.*

*Praise our God, O peoples, let the sound of his praise be heard;*
*He has preserved our lives and kept our feet from slipping.*
*For you, O God, tested us; you refined us like silver.*
*You brought us into prison and laid burdens on our backs*
*You let men ride over our heads;*
*We went through fire and water, but you brought us to a place of abundance.*
*Vows my lips promised and my mouth spoke when I was in trouble.*

*I will sacrifice fat animals to you and offering of rams;*
*I will offer bulls and goats.*

*Come and listen, all you who fear God;*
*Let me tell you what he has done for me.*
*I cried out to him with my mouth; his praise was on my tongue.*
***If I had cherished sin in my heart, the Lord would not have listened;***
*But God has surely listened and heard my voice in prayer.*
*Praise be to God, who has not rejected my prayer*
*Or withheld his love from me!*

## Psalm 67

*May God be gracious to us and bless us and make his face shine upon us;*
*May your ways be known on earth, your salvation among all nations.*

*May the peoples praise you, O God;*
*May all the peoples praise you.*
*May the nations be glad and sing for joy,*
*For you rule the peoples justly and guide the nations of the earth.*
*May the peoples praise you, O God;*
*May all the peoples praise you.*

*Then the land will yield its harvest, and God, our God, will bless us.*
*God will bless us, and all the ends of the earth will fear him.*

## Psalm 68

*May God arise, may his enemies be scattered; may his foes flee before him.*
*As smoke is blown away by the wind, may the wicked perish before God.*

*But may the righteous be glad and rejoice before God;*
*May they be happy and joyful.*
*Sing to God, sing praise to his name,*
*Extol him who rides on the clouds—his name is the Lord--and rejoice before him.*
*A father to the fatherless, a defender of widows, is God in his holy dwelling.*
*God set the lonely in families, he leads forth the prisoners with singing;*
*But the rebellious live in a sun-scorched land. (Psalm 68:1-6)*

*Praise be to the Lord, to God our Savior, who daily bears our burdens.*
*(Psalm 68:19)*

*Your procession has come into view, O God,*
*The procession of my God and King into the sanctuary.*
***In front are the singers, after them the musicians;***
*With them are the maidens playing tambourines.*
*Praise God in the great congregation;*
*Praise the Lord in the assembly of Israel.*
*There is the little tribe of Benjamin, leading them,*

*There the great throng of Judah's princes,*
*And there the princes of Zebulun and of Naphtali. (Psalm 68:24-27)*

*Sing to God, O kingdoms of the earth, sing praise to the Lord,*
*To him who rides the ancient skies above, who thunders with mighty voice.*
*Proclaim the power of God, whose majesty is over Israel,*
*Whose power is in the skies.*
*You are awesome, O God, in your sanctuary;*
***The God of Israel gives power and strength to his people.***
*Praise be to God! (Psalm 68:32-35)*

## Psalm 69

*I will praise God's name in song and glorify him with thanksgiving.*
*This will please the Lord more than an ox,*
*More than a bull with its horns and hoofs. (Psalm 69:30-31)*

*Let heaven and earth praise him, the seas and all that move in them,*
*For God will save Zion and rebuild the cities of Judah.*
*Then people will settle there and possess it;*
*The children of his servants will inherit it,*
*And those who love his name will dwell there. (Psalm 69:34-36)*

## Psalm 70

*But may all who seek you rejoice and be glad in you;*
*May those who love your salvation always say,*
*'Let God be exalted!' (Psalm 70:4)*

## Psalm 71

*My mouth is filled with your praise, declaring your splendor all day long.*
*(Psalm 70:8)*
*But as for me, I will always have hope;*
*I will praise you more and more. (Psalm 71:14)*

*I will praise you with the harp for your faithfulness, O my God;*
*I will sing praise to you with the lyre, O Holy One of Israel.*
*My lips will shout for joy when I sing praise to you--*
*I, whom you have redeemed.*
*My tongue will tell of your righteous acts all day long,*
*For those who wanted to harm me have been put to shame and confusion.*
*(Psalm 71:22-24)*

## Psalm 72

*Praise be to the Lord God, the God of Israel,*
*Who alone does marvelous deeds.*
*Praise be to his glorious name forever;*
*May the whole earth be filled with his glory.*

*Amen and Amen. (Psalm 72:18-19)*

## Psalm 73
*Whom have I in heaven but you?*
*And being with you, I desire nothing on earth. (Psalm 73:25)*

## Psalm 75
*We give thanks to you, O God, we give thanks, for your Name is near;*
*Men tell of your wonderful deeds. (Psalm 75:1)*

*As for me, I will declare this forever;*
*I will sing praise to the God of Jacob.*
*I will cut off the horns of all the wicked,*
*But the horns of the righteous will be lifted up. (Psalm 75:9-10)*

## Psalm 79
*Pay back into the laps of our neighbors seven times the reproach*
*They have hurled at you, O Lord.*
*Then we your people, the sheep of your pasture, will praise you forever;*
*From generation to generation we will recount your praise. (Psalm 79:12-13)*

## Psalm 81
*Sing for joy to God our strength;*
*Shout aloud to the God of Jacob!*
*Begin the music, strike the tambourine,*
*Play the melodious harp and lyre.*
*Sound the ram's horn at the New Moon, and when the moon is full,*
*On the day of our Feast;*
*This is a decree for Israel, and ordinance of the God of Jacob.*
*He established it as a statute for Joseph when he went out against Egypt,*
*Where we heard a language we did not understand. (Psalm 81:1-5)*

## Psalm 84
*How lovely is your dwelling place, O Lord Almighty!*
*My soul yearns, even faints for the courts of the Lord;*
*My heart and my flesh cry out for the Living God. (Psalm 84:1-2)*

*Blessed are those who dwell in your house;*
*They are ever praising you,*
*Blessed are those whose strength is in you,*
*Who have set their hearts on pilgrimage.*
*As they pass through the Valley of Baca, they make it a place of springs;*
*The autumn rains also cover it with pools.*
*They go from strength to strength*
*Till each appears before God in Zion. (Psalm 84:4-7)*

<u>Worship God In Spirit And In Truth</u>

**_Better is one day in your courts than a thousand elsewhere;_**
_I would rather be a doorkeeper in the house of my God_
_Than dwell in the tents of the wicked._
_For the Lord God is a sun and shield;_
_The Lord bestows favor and honor;_
_No good thing does he withhold from those whose walk is blameless._
_O Lord Almighty, blessed is the man who trusts in you. (Psalm 84:10-12)_

## Psalm 87

_As they make music they will sing,_
_'All my fountains are in you.' (Psalm 87)_

## Psalm 89

_I will sing of the Lord's great love forever;_
_With my mouth I will make your faithfulness known through all generations._
_I will declare that your love stands firm forever,_
_That you established your faithfulness in heaven itself. (Psalm 89:1-2)_

_I have found David my servant;_
_With my sacred oil I have anointed Him. (Psalm 89:20)_
The Bride of Christ is anointed with the same sacred oil.

## Psalm 92

**_It is good to praise the Lord_**
_And make music to your name, O Most High,_
_To proclaim your love in the morning_
_And your faithfulness at night,_
_To the music of the ten-stringed lyre_
_And the melody of the harp._

_How great are your works, O Lord,_
_How profound your thoughts!_
_The senseless man does not know,_
_Fools do not understand,_
_That though the wicked spring up like grass_
_And all evildoers flourish,_
_They will be forever destroyed._

_But you, O Lord, are exalted forever._

_For surely your enemies will perish;_
_all evildoers will be scattered._

_You have exalted my horn (strength) like that of a wild ox;_
**_Fine oils have been poured upon me._**

_My eyes have seen the defeat of my adversaries;_

*My ears have heard the rout of my wicked foes.*

*The righteous will flourish like a palm tree,*
*They will grow like a cedar of Lebanon;*
*Planted in the house of the Lord,*
*They will flourish in the courts of our God.*
*They will still bear fruit in old age,*
*They will stay fresh and green,*
*Proclaiming, 'the Lord is upright;*
*He is my Rock, and there is no wickedness in him.' (Psalm 92)*

## Psalm 95

**Come**, *Let us sing for joy to the Lord;*
*Let us shout aloud to the Rock of our salvation.*
*Let us come before him with thanksgiving*
*And extol him with music and song.*

*For the Lord is the great God,*
*The great King above all gods.*
*In his hand are the depths of the earth,*
*And the mountain peaks belong to him.*
*The sea is his, for he made it,*
*And his hands formed the dry land.*

**Come**, *let us bow down in worship,*
*Let us kneel before the Lord our Maker;*
*For he is our God*
*And we are the people of his pasture,*
*The flock under his care. (Psalm 95:1-7)*

## Psalm 96

**Sing to the lord a new song**;
*Sing to the Lord, all the earth.*
*Sing to the Lord, praise his name;*
*Proclaim his salvation day after day.*
*Declare his glory among the nations,*
*His marvelous deeds among all peoples.*

*For great is the Lord and most worthy of praise;*
*He is to be feared above all gods.*
*For all the gods of the nations are idols,*
*But the Lord made the heavens.*
*Splendor and majesty are before him;*
*Strength and glory are in his sanctuary.*

*Ascribe to the Lord, O families of nations,*
*Ascribe to the Lord glory and strength.*

**47**

<u>Worship God In Spirit And In Truth</u>

*Ascribe to the Lord the glory due his name;*
*Bring an offering and come into his courts.*
*Worship the Lord in the splendor of his holiness;*
*Tremble before him, all the earth.*

*Say among the nations, 'the Lord reigns.'*
*The world is firmly established, it cannot be moved;*
*He will judge the peoples with equity.*
*Let the heavens rejoice, let the earth be glad;*
*Let the sea resound, and all that is in it;*
*Let the fields be jubilant, and everything in them.*
*Then all the trees of the forest will sing for joy;*
*They will sing before the Lord,*
*For he comes to judge the world in righteousness*
*And the peoples in his truth. (Psalm 96)*

## Psalm 97
**Rejoice in the Lord**, *you who are righteous,*
*And praise his holy name. (Psalm 97:12)*

## Psalm 98
***Sing to the Lord a new song***,
*For he has done marvelous things;*
*His right hand and his holy arm*
*Have worked salvation for him.*
*The Lord has made his salvation known*
*And revealed his righteousness to the nations.*
*He has remembered his love and his faithfulness to the house of Israel;*
*All the ends of the earth have seen the salvation of our God.*

***Shout for joy to the Lord, all the earth***,
*Burst into jubilant song with music;*
*Make music to the Lord with the harp,*
*With the harp and the sound of singing,*
*With trumpets and the blast of the ram's horn--*
*Shout for joy before the Lord, the King.*

*Let the sea resound, and everything in it,*
*The world, and all who live in it.*
*Let the rivers clap their hands,*
*Let the mountains sing together for joy;*
*Let them sing before the Lord*
*For he comes to judge the earth.*
*He will judge the world in righteousness*
*And the peoples with equity. (Psalm 98)*

## Psalm 100
**Shout for joy to the Lord, all the earth.**
*Serve the lord with gladness;*
*Come before him with joyful songs.*
*Know that the Lord is God.*
*It is he who made us, and we are his;*
*We are the people of his pasture.*

*Enter his gates with thanksgiving and his courts with praise;*
*Give thanks to him and praise his name.*
*For the Lord is good and his love endures forever;*
*His faithfulness continues through all generations. (Psalm 100)*

## Psalm 101
**I will sing of your love and justice**;
*To you O Lord, I will sing praise.*
*I will be careful to lead a blameless life--*
*When will you come to me?*

*I will walk in my house with blameless heart.*
*I will set before my eyes no vile thing. (Psalm 101:1-3)*

## Psalm 102
*So the name of the Lord will be declared in Zion and his praise in Jerusalem*
*When the peoples and the kingdoms assemble to worship the Lord.*
*(Psalm 102:21-22)*

## Psalm 103
**Praise the Lord, O my soul**;
*All my inmost being, praise his holy name.*
*Praise the Lord, O my soul,*
*And forget not all his benefits.*

*He forgives all my sins and heals all my diseases;*
*He redeems my life from the pit*
*And crowns me with love and compassion.*
*He satisfies my desires with good things,*
*So that my youth is renewed like the eagle's. (Psalm 103:1-5)*

## Psalm 104
**Praise the Lord, O my soul.**
*O Lord my God, you are very great;*
*You are clothed with splendor and majesty.*
*He wraps himself in light as with a garment;*
*He stretches out the heavens like a tent*

**49**

<u>Worship God In Spirit And In Truth</u>

And lays the beams of his upper chambers on their waters.
He makes the clouds his chariot
And rides on the wings of the wind.
He makes winds his messengers,
Flames of fire his servants.

He set the earth on its foundations; it can never be moved.
You covered it with the deep as with a garment;
The waters stood above the mountains.
But at your rebuke the waters fled,
At the sound of your thunder they took to flight;
They flowed over the mountains,
They went down into the valleys,
To the place you assigned for them.
You set a boundary they cannot cross;
Never again will they cover the earth.

He makes springs pour water into the ravines;
It flows between the mountains.
They give water to all the beasts of the field;
The wild donkeys quench their thirst.
The birds of the air nest by the waters;
They sing among the branches.
He waters the mountains from his upper chambers;
The earth is satisfied by the fruit of his work.

He makes grass grow for the cattle,
And plants for man to cultivate--
Bringing forth food from the earth:
Wine gladdens the heart of man,
Oil to make his face shine,
And bread that sustains his heart.

The trees of the Lord are well watered,
The cedars of Lebanon that he planted.
There the birds make their nests;
The stork has its home in the pine trees.
The high mountains belong to the wild goats;
The crags are a refuge for the coneys.

The moon marks off the seasons,
And the sun knows when to go down.
You bring darkness, it becomes night,
And all the beasts of the forest prowl.
The lions roar for their prey
And seek their food from God.
The sun rises, and they steal away;

*They return and lie down in their dens.*
*Then man goes out to his work,*
*His labor until evening.*

*How many are your works, O Lord!*
*In wisdom you made them all;*
*The earth is full of your creatures beyond number--*
*Living things both large and small.*
*There the ships go to and fro,*
*And the leviathan, which you formed to frolic there.*

*These all look to you to give them their food at the proper time.*
*When you give it to them, they gather it up;*
*When you open your hand they are satisfied with good things.*
*When you hid your face, they are terrified;*
*When you take away their breath, they die and return to the dust.*
*When you send your Spirit they are created,*
*And you renew the face of the earth.*

*May the glory of the Lord endure forever;*
*May the Lord rejoice in his  works.*
*He looks at the earth, and it trembles;*
*He touches the mountains, and they smoke.*

***I will sing to the Lord all my life;***
***I will sing praise to my God as long as I live.***
*May my meditation be pleasing to him, as I rejoice in the Lord.*
*But may sinners vanish from the earth*
*And the wicked be no more.*
***Praise the Lord, O my soul.***
***Praise the Lord.*** *(Psalm 104)*

## Psalm 105
*Give thanks to the Lord, call on his name;*
*Make known among the nations what he has done.*
*Sing to him, sing praise to him;*
*Tell of all his wonderful acts.*
*Glory in his holy name;*
*Let the hearts of those who seek the Lord rejoice.*
*Look to the Lord and his strength;*
*Seek his face always. (Psalm 105:1-4)*

## Psalm 106
*Praise the Lord.*
*Give thanks to the Lord, for he is good;*
*His love endures forever. (Psalm 106:1)*

<u>Worship God In Spirit And In Truth</u>

*Praise be to the Lord, the God of Israel,*
*From everlasting to everlasting.*
*Let the people say, 'Amen!'*
*Praise the Lord. (Psalm 106:48)*

## Psalm 107
*Give thanks to the Lord, for he is good;*
*His love endures forever. (Psalm 107:1)*

## Psalm 108
*My heart is steadfast, O God;*
*I will sing and make music with all my soul.*
*Awake, harp and lyre! I will awaken the dawn.*
*I will praise you, O Lord, among the nations;*
*I will sing of you among the peoples.*
*For great is your love, higher than the heavens;*
*Your faithfulness reaches to the skies.*
*Be exalted, O God above the heavens,*
*And let your glory be over all the earth. (Psalm 107:1-5)*

## Psalm 109
*O God, whom I praise, do not remain silent,*
*For the wicked and deceitful men have opened their mouths against me;*
*They have spoken against me with lying tongues. (Psalm 109:1-2)*

## Psalm 111
*Praise the lord.*
*I will extol the Lord with all my heart in the council of the upright*
*And in the assembly. (Psalm 111:1)*

## Psalm 112
*Praise the Lord.*
*Blessed is the man who fears the Lord,*
*Who finds great delight in his commands. (Psalm 112:1)*

## Psalm 113
*Praise the Lord.*
*Praise, O servants of the Lord, praise the name of the Lord.*
*Let the name of the Lord be praised, both now and forevermore.*
*From the rising of the sun to the place where it sets*
*The name of the lord is to be praised. (Psalm 113:1-3)*

## Psalm 115
*It is not the dead who praise the lord, those who go down to silence;*
*It is we who extol the Lord, both now and forevermore.*

*Praise the Lord. (Psalm 115:17-18)*

## Psalm 117
*Praise the Lord, all you nations;*
*Extol him, all you peoples.*
*For great is his love toward us,*
*And the faithfulness of the Lord endures forever.*
*Praise the Lord.*

## Psalm 118
*Give thanks to the Lord, for he is good;*
*His love endures forevermore*
*Let Israel say: 'His love endures forever.'*
*Let the house of Aaron say: 'His love endures forever.'*
*Let those who fear the Lord say: 'His love endures forever.' (Psalm 118:1-4)*

*Shouts of joy and victory resound in the tents of the righteous:*
*'The Lord's right hand has done mighty things!*
*The Lord;s right hand is lifted high;*
*The Lord's right hand has done mighty things!' (Psalm 118:15-16)*

*Open for me the gates of righteousness;*
*I will enter and give thanks to the Lord.*
*This is the gate of the Lord*
*Through which the righteous may enter.*
*I will give you thanks, for you answered me;*
*You have become my salvation.*

**The stone the builders rejected has become the capstone;**
**The Lord has done this, and it is marvelous in our eyes.**
*This is the day the Lord has made;*
*Let us rejoice and be glad in it. (Psalm 118:24)*

[The gate of access to the Lord is righteousness
And the righteous go through them to give the Lord thanks
For all that He has done for them.

In every generation builders claim the God of Heaven
But reject the Christ of God.
It is marvelous in our eyes, that they would do such a thing.
Nevertheless, it is our day, unlike any other day, made by God for us,
And we will rejoice and be glad in it.]

*You are my God, and I will give you thanks;*
*You are my God, and I will exalt you.*

*Give thanks to the Lord, for he is good;*

**53**

*His love endures forever. (Psalm 118:28-29)*

## Psalm 119
*I will praise you with an upright heart*
*As I learn your righteous laws.*
*I will obey your decrees; do not utterly forsake me.*

*I have hidden your word in my heart*
*That I might not sin against you.*
*Praise be to you, O Lord; teach me your decrees.*
*With my lips I recount all the laws that come from your mouth.*
*I rejoice in following your statutes as one rejoices in great riches.*
*I meditate on your precepts and consider your ways.*
*I delight in your decrees; I will not neglect your word. (Psalm 119:11-16)*

*Open my eyes that I may see wonderful things in your law.*
***I am a stranger on earth***; *do not hide your commands from me.*
*My soul is consumed with longing for your laws at all times. (Psalm 119:18-20)*

[It is worth noting that in the natural we try to fit into our culture,
However, those who belong to the Lord are strangers on earth;
They are in the world, but not of it.]

*I have chosen the way of truth; I have set my heart on your laws.*
*I hold fast to your statutes, O Lord; Do not let me be put to shame.*
*I run in the path of your commands, for you have set my heart free.*
*(Psalm 119:30-32)*

[Amen. Christ Jesus came to set our hearts free.
Free to be righteous, free to be holy, free to love without conditions.]

*Your decrees are the theme of my song wherever I lodge. (Psalm 119:54)*

*At midnight I rise to give you thanks for your righteous laws. (Psalm 119:62)*

*To all perfection I see a limit;*
*But your commands are boundless. (Psalm 119:96)*

*Your word is a lamp to my feet and a light for my path. (Psalm 119:105)*

*Accept, O Lord, the willing praise of my mouth, and teach me your laws.*
*(Psalm 119:108)*

*Your statutes are my heritage forever; they are the joy of my heart.*
*(Psalm 119:111)*

Worship God In Spirit And In Truth

*My zeal wears me out, for my enemies ignore your words. (Psalm 119:139)*
*Seven times a day I praise you for your righteous laws. (119:164)*
*My lips overflow with praise, for you teach me your decrees.*
*May my tongue sing of your word, for all your commands are righteous.*

*Let me live that I may praise you, and may your laws sustain me. (Psalm 119:175)*

## Psalm 122

*I rejoice with those who said to me, 'Let us go to the house of the Lord.'*
*Our feet are standing in your gates, O Jerusalem.*
*Jerusalem is built like a city that is closely compacted together.*
*That is where the tribes go up, the tribes of the Lord,*
*To praise the name of the Lord according to the statute given to Israel.*
*(Psalm 122:1-4)*

## Psalm 124

*Praise be to the Lord, who has not let us be torn by their teeth.*
*We have escaped like a bird out of the fowler's snare;*
*The snare has been broken, and we have escaped.*
*Our help is in the name of the Lord, the Maker of heaven and earth. (Psalm 124:6)*

## Psalm 126

*When the Lord brought back the captives to Zion,*
*We were like men who dreamed.*
*Our mouths were filled with laughter, our tongues with songs of joy.*
*Then it was said among the nations, 'The Lord has done great things for them.'*
*The Lord has done great things for us, and we are filled with joy.*

*Restore our fortunes, O Lord, like streams in the Negev.*
*Those who sow in tears will reap with songs of joy.*
*He who goes out weeping, carrying seed to sow,*
*Will return with songs of joy, carrying sheaves with him.*

## Psalm 127

*Unless the Lord builds the house, its builders labor in vain.*
*Unless the Lord watches over the city, the watchmen stand guard in vain.*
*(Psalm 127:1)*

## Psalm 132

*O Lord, remember David and all the hardships he endured.*

*He swore an oath to the Lord and made a vow to the Mighty One of Jacob:*
*'I will not enter my house or go to my bed--*
*I will allow no sleep to my eyes, no slumber to my eyelids,*
*Till I find a place for the Lord, a dwelling for the Mighty One of Jacob.'*

Worship God In Spirit And In Truth

[It is interesting that this is how David felt
And yet God found more pleasure in the tent, The Tabernacle of David,
Than in the Temple of Solomon and all its extravagance.
God is looking for extravagant worship not extravagant houses of worship.
Extravagant houses of worship serve men not necessarily God.
The ultimate house of God is the Bride of Christ.
A city built with living stones, the saints of God.]

*We heard it in Ephrathah, we came upon it in the fields of Jaar:*
*'Let us go to his dwelling place; let us worship at his footstool--*
*Arise, O Lord, and come to your resting place,*
*You and the ark of your might.*
*May your priests be clothed with righteousness;*
*May your saints sing for joy.'*
*For the sake of David your servant, do not reject your anointed one.*

*The Lord swore an oath to David, a sure oath that he will not revoke:*
*'One of your own descendants I will place on your throne--*
*If your sons keep my covenant and the statutes I teach them,*
*Then their sons will sit on your throne for ever and ever.'*

*For the Lord has chosen Zion, he has desired it for his dwelling;*
*'This is my resting place for ever and ever;*
*Here I will sit enthroned, for I have desired it--*
*I will bless her with abundant provisions;*
*Her poor will I satisfy with food.*
*I will clothe her priests with salvation,*
*And her saints will ever sing for joy.*

*'Here I will make a horn grow for David*
*And set up a lamp for my anointed one.*
*I will clothe his enemies with shame,*
*But the crown on his head will be resplendent.' (Psalm 132)*

[In every generation, The Bride of Christ,
Has sought to provide a dwelling place for the Lord.
She is the dwelling place He seeks.
Those who worship Him in Spirit and in Truth.]

## Psalm 133
*How good and pleasant it is when brothers live together in unity!*
*It is like precious oil poured on the head, running down on the beard,*
*Running down on Aaron's beard, down upon the collar of his robes.*
*It is as if the dew of Hermon were falling on Mount Zion.*
*For there the Lord bestows his blessing, even life forevermore.*

[On earth unity comes when the people of God

Worship God In Spirit And In Truth

Worship their God in Spirit and in Truth.
They are then made ONE by the power of the Spirit;
They, then become Zion, the City of God, The New Jerusalem, The Bride of Christ.
It is there that the Lord bestows His blessing, even LIFE forevermore!]

## Psalm 134
*Praise the Lord, all you servants of the Lord*
*Who minister by night in the house of the Lord.*
*Lift up your hands in the sanctuary and praise the Lord.*
*May the Lord, the maker of heaven and earth, bless you from Zion.*

[Ultimately the only place of blessing is Zion, The City of God.]

## Psalm 135
*Praise the Lord.*

*Praise the name of the Lord;*
*Praise him, you servants of the Lord,*
*You who minister in the house of the Lord,*
*In the courts of the house of our God.*

*Praise the Lord, for the Lord is good;*
*Sing praise to his name, for that is pleasant.*
*For the Lord has chosen Jacob to be his own,*
*Israel to be his treasured possession. (Psalm 135:1-4)*

[This Israel spoken of here is, The Israel of God, Zion, The City of God,
The Bride of Christ, the only lasting possession of God,
Which includes those from natural Israel who are faithful to Him.]

*O house of Israel, praise the Lord;*
*O house of Aaron, praise the Lord;*
*O house of Levi, praise the Lord;*
*You who fear him, praise the Lord.*
*Praise be to the Lord from Zion,*
*To him who dwells in Jerusalem.*

*Praise the Lord. (Psalm 135:19-21)*

## Psalm 136
*Give thanks to the Lord, for he is good.*
        *His love endures forever.*
*Give thanks to the God of gods.*
        *His love endures forever.*
*Give thanks to the Lord of lords.*
        *His love endures forever. (Psalm 136:1-3)*

Worship God In Spirit And In Truth

*Give thanks to the God of heaven.*
*His love endures forever. (Psalm 136:26)*

## Psalm 138

*I will praise you, O Lord, with all my heart;*
*Before the 'gods' I will sing your praise.*
*I will bow down toward your holy temple and will praise your name*
*For your love and your faithfulness,*
**For you have exalted above all things your name and your word.**
*When I called, you answered me;*
*You made me bold and stouthearted.*

*May all the kings of the earth praise you, O Lord,*
*When they hear the words of your mouth.*
*May they sing of the ways of the Lord,*
*For the glory of the Lord is great. (Psalm 138:1-5)*

## Psalm 139

*I praise you because I am fearfully and wonderfully made;*
*Your works are wonderful, I know that full well. (Psalm 139:14)*

## Psalm 140

*Surely the righteous will praise your name*
*And the upright will live before you. (Psalm 140:13)*

## Psalm 142

*Set me free from my prison, that I may praise your name.*
*Then the righteous will gather about me*
*Because of your goodness to me.*

## Psalm 143

*Show me the way I should go, for to you I lift up my soul.*
*Rescue me from my enemies O Lord,*
**For I hide myself in you.**
*Teach me to do your will, for you are my God;*
*May your good Spirit lead me on level ground.*

## Psalm 144

*Praise be to the Lord my Rock, who trains my hands for battle. (Psalm 144:1)*

[The Lord trains the righteous to worship in Spirit and in Truth,
Clad in the full armor of God,
To destroy all the work of the enemy through Christ in them,
His ultimate instrument of battle.]

<u>Worship God In Spirit And In Truth</u>

*I will sing a new song to you O God;*
*On the ten-stringed lyre I will make music to you,*
*To the One who gives victory to kings,*
*Who delivers his servant David from the deadly sword. (Psalm 144:9)*

## Psalm 145

*I will exalt you, my God the King;*
*I will praise your name for ever and ever.*
*Every day I will praise you and extol your name for ever and ever.*
*Great is the Lord and most worthy of praise;*
***His greatness no one can fathom.***
*One generation will commend your works to another;*
*They will tell of your mighty acts.*
*They will speak of the glorious splendor of your majesty,*
*And I will meditate on your wonderful works.*
*They will tell of the power of your awesome works,*
*And I will proclaim your great deeds.*
*They will celebrate your abundant goodness*
*And joyfully sing of your righteousness.*

*The Lord is gracious and compassionate,*
*Slow to anger and rich in love.*
*The Lord is good to all;*
*He has compassion on all he has made.*
*All you have made will praise you, O Lord;*
*Your saints will extol you.*
*They will tell of the glory of your kingdom*
*And speak of your might,*
*So that all men may know of your mighty acts*
*And the glorious splendor of your kingdom,*
*And your dominion endures through all generations.*

*The Lord is faithful to all his promises*
*And loving toward all he has make.*
*The Lord upholds all those who fall*
*And lifts up all who are bowed down.*
*The eyes of all look to you,*
*And you give them their food at the proper time.*
*You open your hand*
*And satisfy the desires of every living thing.*

***The Lord is near to all who call on him,***
***To all who call on him in truth.***
*He fulfills the desires of those who fear him;*
*He hears their cry and saves them.*
*The Lord watches over all who love him,*
*But the wicked he will destroy.*

## Worship God In Spirit And In Truth

*My mouth will speak in praise of the Lord.*
*Let every creature praise his holy name for ever and ever.*

## Psalm 146
*Praise the Lord.*
*Praise the Lord, O my soul.*
*I will praise the Lord all my life;*
*I will sing praise to my God as long as I live. (Psalm 146:1-2)*

*The Lord reigns forever, your God, O Zion, for all generations.*
*Praise the Lord. (Psalm 146:10)*

## Psalm 147
*Praise the Lord.*
*How good it is to sing praises to our God,*
*How pleasant and fitting to praise him!*

*The Lord builds up Jerusalem;*
*He gathers the exiles of Israel.*
*He heals the brokenhearted and binds up their wounds.*

*He determines the number of stars and calls them each by name.*
*Great is our Lord and mighty is power;*
*His understanding has no limit.*
*The Lord sustains the humble but casts the wicked to the ground.*

*Sing to the Lord with thanksgiving;*
*Make music to our God on the harp.*
*He covers the sky with clouds;*
*He supplies the earth with rain*
*And makes grass grow on the hills.*
*He provides food for the cattle*
*And for the young ravens when they call.*

*His pleasure is not in the strength of the horse,*
*Nor his delight in the legs of a man;*
*The Lord delights in those who fear him,*
*Who put their hope in his unfailing love.*

*Extol the Lord, O Jerusalem;*
*Praise your God, O Zion,*
*For he strengthens the bars of your gates*
*And blesses your people within you.*
*He grants peace to your borders*
*And satisfies you with the finest of wheat.*

*He sends his command to the earth;*
*His word runs swiftly.*
*He spreads the snow like wool*
*And scatters the frost like ashes.*
*He hurls down his hail like pebbles.*
*Who can withstand his icy blast?*
*He sends his word and melts them;*
*He stirs up his breezes, and the waters flow.*

*He has revealed his word to Jacob,*
*His laws and decrees to Israel.*
***He has done this for no other nation;***
*They do not know his laws.*

*Praise the Lord.*

## Psalm 148
*Praise the Lord.*

*Praise the Lord from the heavens,*
*Praise him in the heights above.*
*Praise him, all his angels,*
*Praise him, all his heavenly hosts.*
*Praise him, sun and moon,*
*Praise him, all you shining stars.*
*Praise him, you highest heavens*
*And you waters above the skies.*
*Let them praise the name of the Lord,*
*For he commanded and they were created.*
*He set them in place for ever and ever;*
*He gave a decree that will never pass away.*

*Praise the Lord from the earth, you great sea creatures*
*And all ocean depths,*
*Lightning and hail, snow and clouds,*
*Stormy winds that do his bidding.*
*You mountains and all hills,*
*Fruit trees and all cedars,*
*Wild animals and all cattle,*
*Small creatures and flying birds,*
*Kings of the earth and all nations,*
*You princes and all rulers on earth,*
*Young men and maidens,*
*Old men and children.*

*Let them praise the name of the Lord,*
***For his name alone is exalted;***

*His splendor is above the earth and the heavens.*
*He has raise up for his people a horn,*
*The praise of all his saints, of Israel,*
*The people close to his heart.*
*Praise the Lord.*
[The "horn" raised up for us in these "last days" is Christ Jesus in us.]

## Psalm 149
*Praise the Lord.*
*Sing to the Lord a new song,*
*His praise in the assembly of the saints.*
*Let Israel rejoice in their Maker;*
*Let the people of Zion be glad in their King.*
*Let them praise his name with dancing*
*And make music to him with tambourine and harp.*
*For the Lord takes delight in his people;*
*He crowns the humble with salvation.*
**Let the saints rejoice in this honor**.
*And sing for joy on their beds.*

*May the praise of God be in their mouths*
*And a double-edged sword in their hands,*
***To inflict vengeance on the nations***
***And punishment on the peoples,***
***To bind their kings with fetters,***
***Their nobles with shackles of iron,***
***To carry out the sentence written against them.***
***This is the glory of all his saints.***

This is what worship in Spirit and in Truth accomplishes in the heavenlies;
This is the glory of those who will enter into this realm, filled with Christ.
This is the joy of The Bride of Christ.

## Psalm 150
*Praise the Lord.*
*Praise God in his sanctuary;*
*Praise him in his mighty heavens.*
*Praise him for his acts of power;*
*Praise him for his surpassing greatness.*
*Praise him with the sounding of the trumpet,*
*Praise him with the harp and lyre,*
*Praise him with tambourine and dancing,*
*Praise him with the strings and flute,*
*Praise him with the clash of cymbals,*
*Praise him with resounding cymbals.*
*Let everything that has breath praise the Lord. Praise the Lord.*

# Worship Excerpts From The New Testament

## Living Sacrifices

*Therefore, I urge you, brothers, in view of God's mercy,*
*To offer your bodies as living sacrifices, holy and pleasing to God—*
*Which is your spiritual worship.*
*Do not conform any longer to the pattern of this world,*
*But be transformed by the renewing of your mind.*
*Then you will be able to test and approve what God's will is--*
*His good, pleasing and perfect will. (Romans 12:1-2)*

In the New Covenant everything we do in our bodies
Is to be consecrated to God; our bodies being a living sacrifice,
As the body of Christ Jesus was a living sacrifice for us.

## A Call To Persevere

**Therefore, brothers,**
**Since we have confidence to enter the Most Holy Place**
**By the blood of Jesus, by a new and living way**
*Opened for us through the curtain, that is his body,*
*And since we have a great priest over the house of God,*
*Let us draw near to God with a sincere heart in full assurance of faith,*
*Having our hearts sprinkled to cleanse us from a guilty conscience*
*And having our bodies washed with pure water.*
*Let us hold unswervingly to the hope we profess,*
*For he who promised is faithful.*
*And let us consider how we may spur one another toward love and good deeds.*
*Let us not give up meeting together, as some are in the habit of doing,*
*But let us encourage one another—*
*And all the more as you see the Day approaching. (Hebrews 10:19-25)*

We can enter the Most Holy Place, having been made a priest;
Having removed our old garments and putting on the garments of Christ;
Being washed in water and sprinkled with the blood of Christ Jesus;
Being filled with the Holy Spirit, the new and Living Way.

We then gather together to worship our great God in His Spirit and in His Truth;
We become ONE with Christ Jesus and the Father by the power of the Spirit,
And the Kingdom of God comes to earth as in Heaven;
Then the will of the Father is done on earth as in Heaven,
And the works of the devil destroyed.

## ABOUT THE AUTHOR

Tom Haeg is an architect, writer, song writer and musician
Who has been a student of the Bible for more than 25 years.
He and his wife Susan have been blessed
To experience the outpouring of God's Spirit called "Renewal"
And have witnessed the manifest presence of God.
Tom and Susan's lives have been changed forever
By this encounter with the Living God;
Changed by His grace, love and power.

They have led worship in small groups and larger services
Where God has poured out His Spirit in marvelous ways.
Through this outpouring they have seen God change lives.

Tom has read extensively about the history of the Christian Church
And the revivals that God has visited upon His people
Up to and including this present time.
He believes that the Final Revival lies dead ahead,
Where God is going to pour out His Spirit in a magnitude
That has never been seen before.
Tom believes that this outpouring will precede The Great Tribulation
Spoken of in the Book of Revelation.
He believes that soon there will be thousands upon thousands of Christians
Ministering Christ Jesus in the power and fullness of Christ.
The name of Jesus will be upon every heart, mind and mouth
Every man woman and child
In every nation on the face of the earth.

Christ Jesus will present Himself personally to every living person on earth.
Every person will be given the opportunity to accept Him
As their Savior, Lord and Anointing.

Tom's previous books are Called By Christ To Be ONE,
The Time Of The END, and The Season Of The Last Generation.
Tom's blog is calledbychristtobeone.blogspot.com.

*The Scriptures used in this book are from the New International Version and
typically italicized. Words in parentheses (and not italicized) are the interpretation of
the author. The author also bolds and underlines Scriptures for the emphasis he
believes of special importance.

CPSIA information can be obtained at www.ICGtesting.com
Printed in the USA
BVOW06s1435071014

369853BV00007B/187/P